JAR 2

D0997280

More
Amazing and Extraordinary
Railway
Facts

David and Charles

More
Amazing and Extraordinary
Railway
Facts

JULIAN HOLLAND

A DAVID & CHARLES BOOK
Copyright © David & Charles Limited 2010

David & Charles is an F+W Media Inc. company
4700 East Galbraith Road
Cincinnati, OH 45236

First published in the UK in 2010

Text copyright © Julian Holland 2010
Illustrations copyright © see page 128

Julian Holland has asserted his right to be identified as author of this
work in accordance with the Copyright, Designs and Patents Act, 1988.

The publisher has endeavoured to contact all contributors of images
for permission to reproduce. If there are any errors or omissions
please send notice in writing to David & Charles Ltd, who will be
happy to make any amendments in subsequent printings.

A catalogue record for this book is available from the British Library.

ISBN-13: 978-0-7153-3622-9 hardback
ISBN-10: 0-7153-3622-3 hardback

Printed in China by RR Donnelley
for David & Charles
Brunel House, Newton Abbot, Devon

Commissioning Editor: Neil Baber
Editor: Verity Muir
Designer: Victoria Marks
Project Editor: Emily Pitcher
Production Controller: Kelly Smith
Pre Press: Natasha Jorden

David & Charles publish high quality books on a wide range of
subjects. For more great book ideas visit: www.rubooks.co.uk

Contents

More Amazing & Extraordinary Railway Facts

Readers of *Amazing & Extraordinary Railway Facts* should know by now that there seems to be no limit to the amount of fascinating facts and stories to be told about Britain's railways. The subject is an enormous treasure chest of information that is seemingly endless so, the publication of this second book should come as no surprise.

As readers are also aware by now, I have a deep-seated love of Britain's railways that stems from a childhood and formative years spent

surrounded by them. Railways are definitely in my blood! As a teenager, at a time when I probably should have been swotting for my GCEs, I spent most of my free time hanging around stations and engine sheds, notebook and camera in hand. Trainspotting trips were planned with military precision and, as I grew older, the destinations grew more distant and, to me, more exotic. For a lad brought up in the West Country my first visit to Polmadie engine shed in Glasgow and St Margaret's in Edinburgh in 1964 was an unforgettable experience. Never before had I seen so many 'foreign' steam locos – I can still remember the smell of oil, steam and smoke that pervaded these hallowed places.

On my trips I was also lucky to also travel over lines that were soon to close and disappear forever – revisiting their ghosts today is an unnerving experience! The list is like a memorial to long-lost friends: the Somerset & Dorset Joint Railway, Barnstaple to Taunton, the Lyme Regis branch, the Stratford-upon-Avon & Midland Junction line. the Great Central main line, the Woodhead line, East Anglian branch lines, the Waverley Route, Dumfries to Stranraer – the list goes on and on.

Sadly, today, I find our railways both clinical (all health and safety nonsense) and incredibly expensive to use. The proliferation of railway operating companies with their garish liveries is an obvious outcome of privatisation but, despite this, many rural lines, particularly in Wales and Scotland, only survive thanks to subsidies from the taxpayer.

One more fascinating fact – I recently discovered on a trip to the far north of Scotland that it takes no less than 40 minutes to cover the 14¼-mile journey between Georgemas Junction and Wick (an average speed of just over 20mph). Why? Well, the two-car Class 158 DMU from Inverness reverses at Georgemas and makes a return journey to Thurso before continuing on to Wick. In 1964, during diesel loco-hauled days, the trip took on average 19 minutes because the train divided at Georgemas Junction. Progress indeed!

The Cornish Riviera Limited

High-speed services to the West Country

Through trains from London Paddington to Penzance were introduced in 1867, with a journey time of around nine hours. Until 1906 trains from Paddington to Devon and Cornwall had to travel the 'Great Way Round' via Bristol, but with the opening of new lines between Patney & Chirton to Westbury in 1900, and from Castle Cary to Cogload Junction (near Taunton) in 1906, the journey was shortened by just over 20 miles. New track bypassing Westbury and Frome opened in 1933, further reducing travelling times.

The 'Cornish Riviera Express' – simply known as the 'Limited' to railway workers – initially ran via Bristol, but in 1906 it took the shorter route via Castle Cary. Slip coaches were included to serve other popular holiday destinations such as Weymouth, Ilfracombe and Newquay. The train became so popular with holidaymakers that it ran in two portions on summer Saturdays until World War I, when it was suspended.

The train resumed service in 1919 and in 1923 the introduction of new carriages and the 'Castle' Class locomotives saw a further improvement in service. The introduction

> **DID YOU KNOW?**
> In 1904 GWR held a competition to find a name for the daily premier express between Paddington and Penzance. The prize was three guineas, and there were over 1,200 entries.

of the more powerful 'King' Class locos in 1927 allowed heavier trains to reach Plymouth in four hours and, two years later, the Great Western Railway (GWR) added through coaches for Falmouth and St Ives. In 1935 new 'Centenary' carriages were introduced and the regular 10.30

departure from Paddington carried reserved seat passengers only and ran (officially) non-stop to Truro – in fact the train halted at Devonport to change engines, the 'King' being too heavy to cross the Royal Albert Bridge. On summer Saturdays such was the demand for the train that it ran 'non-stop' to St Erth with passengers for Falmouth and Helston being conveyed in a relief express.

By 1939 the 'Limited' normally consisted of eight portions: the main portion with restaurant car for Penzance, one through coach each for St Ives, Falmouth, Newquay, Kingsbridge, the Taunton slip with coaches for Ilfracombe and Minehead and the two Weymouth coaches slipped

at Westbury. The train continued to run during World War II but via Bristol, and it wasn't until 1955 that pre-war schedules had been regained. Steam haulage was ousted in the late 1950s with the introduction of 'Warship' Class diesel hydraulics followed in the 1960s by the more powerful 'Western' Class locos. By the end of the decade the journey time to Penzance had come down to 5hr 35min and more was in the pipeline – following haulage for some years by Class 47 and Class 50 diesel electrics the 'Cornish Riviera' (as it was then known) became an HST working in 1979, and by 1983 Plymouth was reached in 3hr 13min and Penzance in 4hr 55min. The ageing HSTs still operate this service.

The Cheltenham Flyer

Record-breaking acceleration from Swindon

During the 1920s and 1930s there was fierce rivalry not only between the British 'Big Four' railway companies, but also among railways throughout the world to lay claim that they ran the fastest scheduled passenger service in the world. For many years the GWR had run the 'Cheltenham Spa Express' between Cheltenham and Paddington, but the introduction of Collett's 'Castle' Class 4-6-0s in 1923 led to a rapid speed up of this service and a change of name to 'Cheltenham Flyer'. Timings were increasingly accelerated until 1929 when the 77¼ miles between Swindon and Paddington was scheduled to take only 70 minutes at an average speed of 66.2mph. In 1931 the timing for Swindon to Paddington was further accelerated to an average speed of 69.2mph, but by now the tantalising 70mph average speed was within the GWR's reach.

On June 6, 1932 Driver Ruddock and Fireman Thorp of Old Oak Common shattered all previous timings and broke all railway speed records. Headed by No. 5006 'Tregenna Castle', the 'Cheltenham Flyer' left the town of its name promptly at 2.30pm and, after a leisurely journey through the Cotswolds, reached Swindon for its final stop before Paddington. At 3.48pm 'Tregenna Castle' and its six coaches left Swindon, and then the fireworks started – the train accelerated continuously until Didcot (24.2 miles from Swindon), and passed in 18min 55sec at a speed of over 90mph. This speed was maintained for mile after mile and, despite a slight slowing past Twyford, the train was travelling at 84.4mph just two miles short of Paddington, which was reached in 56min 47sec from Swindon at an average speed of 81.6mph. What a journey! Three months later the 'Cheltenham Flyer' was accelerated again and rescheduled to take only 65 minutes between Swindon and Paddington at an average speed of 71.3mph – it was now officially the fastest scheduled train in the world.

Hi-Di-Hi!!!

The railway camping coach

By the 1930s the popularity of the great outdoors with the urban masses had make hiking and camping a boom business. Keen to take advantage of this new craze, Britain's 'Big Four' railway companies began providing 'camping coaches' parked in a siding at rural or coastal stations.

In 1933 the London & North Eastern Railway (LNER) became the first to provide camping coaches when they adapted ten redundant ex-Great Northern Railway (GNR) six-wheeler carriages and placed them at ten different beauty spots across their system. Not to be outdone, the GWR and the London, Midland and Scottish Railway (LMS) followed suit the following year, followed by the Southern Railway in 1935. Adapted bogie carriages were later introduced that could sleep up to eight people.

Camping coaches were suspended for the duration of World War II but were reintroduced in 1947. Under British Railways the number of camping locations increased dramatically, with some popular destinations offering a whole row of camping coaches. More luxurious accommodation was also offered in the shape of adapted Pullman coaches, and by 1957 there were over 120 locations on offer from Glenfinnan in Scotland to St Erth in Cornwall – the Western Region alone had 44 locations, mainly in Wales and the West Country.

Sadly, changing holiday habits and the fairly spartan accommodation on offer led to the demise of camping coaches in 1971. A few entrepreneurs have since offered refurbished coaches at railway stations such as St Germans and Hayle in Cornwall.

It's a Small World

The miniature railways of W J Bassett-Lowke and Henry Greenly

W J Bassett-Lowke (1877–1953)

The model company founded in Northampton at the end of the 19th century by Wenman Joseph Bassett-Lowke became a leading sub-contractor and distributor of scale model ships and railways for over 50 years. By the beginning of World War I the company, working closely with model railway engineer Henry Greenly, was offering a range of well-detailed railway models, from 15-inch gauge to Gauge '2', Gauge '1' and the increasingly popular '0' gauge. A whole range of British outline model trains were built for Bassett-Lowke by the German company, Bing,

RAILWAY SMASH.

These sets of two Passenger Cars and one Brake Van (Passenger Cars shown in illustration) are so constructed that when a collision occurs they fly to pieces, being fixed together with springs, which the collision releases. A very realistic effect is produced.

These Cars can be fixed together and used any number of times.

and the French company Carette – many of these faithful reproductions of their full-size counterparts and powered by steam or clockwork. In 1923 Bassett-Lowke also introduced the first '00' gauge table-top railway – versions were available with clockwork or third-rail electric power. These were first manufactured by Bing and then, after that company's demise in 1932, by Trix.

Bassett-Lowke also built complete miniature railways such as the Gauge 1 layout at the Bekonscot Model Village in Beaconsfield, and larger 15-inch gauge locomotives for miniature railways such as the Ravenglass & Eskdale Railway in Cumbria. The latter line was converted by Bassett-Lowke from 3ft-gauge in 1915 and operated using that company's 4-4-2 'Sans Pareil.'

Bassett-Lowke's fortunes declined after World War II and the company closed in 1965. The name was bought by Corgi in 1996 and is currently owned by Hornby, which has restarted production of detailed '0' gauge locomotives and rolling stock.

Henry Greenly (1876–1947)

Born in Birkenhead, Henry Greenly trained as a draughtsman at the Neasden Works of the Metropolitan Railway and went on to become a leading designer of miniature passenger-carrying railways. By the early 20th century he had become a much sought-after consultant model engineer and, as such, worked closely with W J Bassett-Lowke designing miniature steam locomotives.

Perhaps Greenly's greatest moment was when he teamed up with millionaire Captain 'Jack' Howey as Chief Engineer of the 13½-mile 18in-gauge Romney, Hythe & Dymchurch Railway, which opened in 1927. Built by Davey-Paxman, his one-third scale steam locomotives still operate on the line today and are a living testimony to his skill as a miniature locomotive designer.

Railways that Never Were

Scottish light railways that were never built

During the latter part of the 19th century and the early years of the 20th a surprising number of hair-brained schemes were put forward to build new railway lines in the sparsely populated region of northwest Scotland and on some of the Western Isles. Despite much optimism from promoters about their future prospects, if built, the lines would never have returned a profit.

The first scheme was the Garve & Ullapool Railway which received authorisation in 1890 to build a 32-mile line from Garve, on the Dingwall & Skye Railway, to the fishing village of Ullapool on the west coast. Nothing came of this due to lack of capital, but it was revived a couple of years later by the Great North of Scotland Railway – their nearest railhead was at Elgin and to work the Ullapool line the company would have needed to obtain running powers over the existing Highland Railway line between that town and Garve via Inverness and Dingwall. Naturally the Highland Railway would have none of this and the scheme quietly died. A similar fate befell a scheme to build a 35-mile line from Achnasheen, also on the Dingwall & Ske Railway, to Gairloch and Aultbea.

The passing of the Light Railways Act in 1896 brought about hundreds of schemes to build low cost railways in rural areas throughout Great Britain and Ireland. Taking advantage of the

> ### DID YOU KNOW?
> A 19-mile gauge line was proposed from Dingwall to Cromarty and the first six miles was actually built in 1914 – then along came World War I and the line was abandoned. Its route can still be seen today.

provisions within the Act, the Highland Railway was quick off the mark and within a year the company had put forward an ambitious programme for the building of nearly 250 miles of new lines in the region. These included reviving the already proposed lines to Ullapool and Aultbea, a

41-mile line from Culrain on the Inverness to Far North line, to Lochinver and a 42-mile line from Lairg to Loch Laxford. All of these schemes were designed to provide an outlet for the west coast's fishing industry, provide new links with ferries to the Outer Hebrides and take advantage of the up-and-coming tourist industry. Probably fortunately for the Highland Railway, none of them ever saw the light of day!

In the far northeast of Scotland the company also proposed building new lines from Forsinard to Melvich and Portskerra (14 miles), from Thurso to Scrabster and also to Gills Bay (17 miles) and from Wick to Dunbeath (20 miles). Of these only the line to Lybster (7 miles north of Dunbeath) was built. Apart from the branch line from The Mound to Dornoch, another scheme further down the east coast from Fearn to Portmahomack (9 miles) also never materialised.

Narrow gauge railways with a 3ft 6in gauge were also proposed by the Highland Railway on the Hebridean islands of Lewis, Harris and Skye. On Lewis and Harris proposals included lines from Stornoway west to Carloway and Dunan Pier and south to Tarbert. On Skye, lines were to be built from Kyleakin to Torrin, and from Isleornsay in the south to Broadford, Portree and Uig in the north with a branch to Dunvegan. None of these lines were ever built.

Silver Service

Railway restaurant cars

The introduction of dining cars on Britain's railways dates back to November 1879, when the Great Northern Railway (GNR) introduced the first vehicle of its kind seen in this country on its London to Leeds service. The Midland Railway (MR) followed suit by putting dining cars on its competing London to Leeds service in 1882, and within a short time the three competing routes from London to Manchester (L&NWR, MR, GNR) all had similar accommodation. The longer Anglo-Scottish routes didn't receive this service until 1893 due to the vested interests of refreshment rooms at Preston, York and Normanton, where passengers usually alighted to take lunch before resuming their journey.

The GWR found themselves in a difficult situation as a 99-year agreement had been made with a catering company in 1842, whereby all of their trains had to stop at Swindon for ten minutes for refreshments. By the 1890s the GWR found this an intolerable situation and in 1895 bought out the Swindon

Junction Hotel Company for £100,000. Dining cars soon appeared on the GWR after this date.

By the early 20th century the provision of dining cars was greatly facilitated by the introduction of corridor trains – this allowed more passengers to be fed in comfort with less plant and staff. On short journeys it was often necessary to provide accommodation for feeding a large

number of passengers simultaneously – the Great Eastern Railway's 'Harwich Boat Express' occupied a journey of only an hour and a half but in that time was able to serve meals to 111 passengers from a kitchen measuring only 6ft x 17ft in the centre of the train. While the greater part of the food consumed on restaurant cars was cooked in the tiny confines of the on-train kitchen, some items such as soup, pastry and sweets were usually prepared beforehand at railway-owned hotels. The Great Eastern Hotel at Liverpool Street baked bread and pastry for restaurant cars and

refreshment rooms down the GER main line; the L&NWR had a bakery at Euston and Rugby and the GNR at Peterborough. By 1904 the railway restaurant car business was booming – the L&NWR/Caledonian Railway served over 500,000 meals annually in its West Coast Joint vehicles between Euston and Glasgow.

130 years after being introduced the last few surviving restaurant car services in the UK on the ECML between King's Cross and Edinburgh are threatened with possible withdrawal to make room for additional passengers. Yet more modern progress!

The Table-top Railway

The complicated life and times of Hornby Dublo, Rovex and Triang

The first '00' gauge table-top railway was produced by the German company, Bing, in 1923 and sold in Britain by Bassett-Lowke (see page 12). However, it was Hornby Trains that first introduced the mass-market range known as Hornby Dublo in 1938. Owned by the famous Liverpool firm Meccano, Hornby Trains had become a household name in the 1920s and '30s with their '0' Gauge tinplate train sets.

When introduced the Hornby Dublo range consisted of die-cast locomotives, tin plate wagons and coaches and tin-plate track with a 12V DC third-rail for electrical pick-up. Clockwork locos were also available until production ceased in World War II. Production resumed in 1948 but, within a decade, the heavy diecast locos and unrealistic three-rail tin plate track were a thing of the past. By the late 1950s their competitors, notably Tri-ang-Rovex, were producing '00' gauge trains that were made of plastic and ran on two-rail track. Not only were they cheaper than Hornby-Dublo but the quality and detailing of their plastic locos and rolling stock was improving all the time. Left behind in the 'realism' stakes, rather belatedly Hornby introduced two-rail track and plastic rolling stock in 1959. New models were introduced which were a vast improvement on what had gone before, and readers will probably have fond memories of their 'Duchess of Montrose', Stanier '8F' and 'Castle' Class steam locos and Type 1 and Metrovick diesels. The range struggled on for a few more years until 1964 when the parent company, Meccano Ltd, was taken over by

Lines Brothers, the manufacturers of Tri-ang Railways. It was a sad end to a company that had been founded by Frank Hornby in 1901 and that had brought so much joy to boys of all ages for over 60 years.

Tri-ang Railways had its beginnings in the post-war years when Rovex Plastics was formed to make toys for Marks & Spencer. An electric '00' gauge train set was first sold for £2 17s 6d in 1950 – the boxed set consisted of a model 'Princess Elizabeth' 4-6-2 loco, two coaches and a circle of two-rail track. The loco, rolling stock and track bases were made from plastic (cellulose acetate). Although crude by today's standards, the set was a success and was sold for half the price of rival Hornby-Dublo train sets. The following year Rovex Plastics was taken over by Lines Brothers, makers of Tri-ang toys and the '00' gauge range was marketed as Tri-ang Railways. In 1953 the company's name was changed to Rovex Scale Models and the following year production was started at a new factory in Margate. The Tri-ang '00' range went from strength to strength and in 1957 the company also introduced a range of the smaller 'TT' (3mm scale) train sets.

The story of British table-top railways went full circle in 1964 when Lines Brothers, owners of Tri-ang, purchased Meccano Ltd, makers of Hornby Dublo. Originally marketed as Tri-ang-Hornby, the Tri-ang label was soon dropped and their model trains since then have been known as Hornby Railways. With its headquarters still in Margate, and manufacturing now in China, Hornby Railways has also acquired many other famous model-making companies in recent years such as Lima, Rivarossi, Arnold, Airfix, Humbrol and Corgi. The company's turnover in 2007 was nearly £47 million.

Attention!

The military names of locomotives

The naming of locomotives has been popular since the early railways. Names ranging from abbeys, Arthurian legends and the British Empire to castles, fox hunts, monarchs and schools that adorned many steam locomotives lent further glamour to the already-perceived romanticism of rail travel. The GWR's large brass nameplates were a work of art in themselves.

Giving military names to locomotives became a regular practice after World War I when 25 North British Railway's 'C' Class 0-6-0s were named after generals and sites of battles after returning from active duty in northern France. The height of engine naming came in the 1930s and 1940s. The practice continued after Nationalisation, with the naming of whole classes of Western Region mainline diesel locomotives after famous warships.

(Note: BR numbering is used throughout.)

LONDON MIDLAND & SCOTTISH RAILWAY

'Black Five' – four of this class (45154-45158) were given names of Scottish regiments.

'Patriot' Class – military names (including regiments and VC holders) were given in a very haphazard manner to around one-third of the 52 locos of this class.

'Jubilee' Class – despite many of this class being named after colonies of the British Empire, 48 (Nos 45639-45686) were named after famous admirals and sea battles and 44 (Nos 45687-45730) were named after famous British warships.

'Royal Scot' Class – when originally built this class had a mix of regimental names and names of famous L&NWR locomotives. By the mid-'30s all of the class carried regimental names except the last three – 46168 'The Girl Guide', 46169 'The Boy Scout' and 46170 'British Legion'.

LONDON & NORTH EASTERN RAILWAY

'V2' Class – four locos were named after north-eastern regiments (Nos. 60809, 60835, 60872, 60964)

'J36' Class – 25 of these 0-6-0 locos were given names of World War I generals and sites of battles. Unlike other named engines the names were only painted onto the wheel arch and these disappeared over time.

SOUTHERN RAILWAY

'Lord Nelson' Class – the entire class of 16 (30850–30865) was named after famous admirals

'Battle of Britain' Class – Nos. 34049–34090 and 34109/34110 were named after World War II RAF fighter squadrons, airfields and military leaders.

GREAT WESTERN RAILWAY

'Castle' Class – 11 were renamed after World War II military aeroplanes (Nos. 5071–5082). Their original names were given to newer 7000 series locos when built. No. 5017 was renamed in 1954 after the Gloucestershire Regiment following its famous exploits in the Korean War.

BRITISH RAILWAYS STEAM LOCOMOTIVES

'Britannia' Class – five of this class (70040-70044) were given names of former army commanders and No. 70048 was later named 'The Territorial army 1908–1958'

BRITISH RAILWAYS MAIN LINE DIESEL LOCOS

BR Sulzer Type 4 (Class 45) – 25 were named after regiments.
BR Sulzer Type 4 (Class 46) – only one of these, D163/46026, was named 'Leicestershire and Derbyshire Yeomanry'.
North British Type 4 'Warship' – all five (D600-D604) were named after famous warships.

BR/NBR Type 4 'Warship' (Class 42/43) – apart from D800, all the remaining 70 locos were named after famous warships.
English Electric Type 5 ('Deltic'/Class 55) – 14 were named after Scottish and north-eastern regiments.
English Electric Type 4 (Class 50) – the entire class of 50 were named after warships in 1978.

Blue Streak

The short-lived Blue Pullman trains of the 1960s

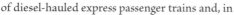

In 1954 the British Transport Commission became the proud owners of the British Pullman Car Company. A year later, the British Railways Modernisation Programme was published – one of its main objectives was the replacement of steam by diesel power. A committee was soon set up to look into the introduction of diesel-hauled express passenger trains and, in 1957, it was announced that the Metropolitan-Cammel Carriage & Wagon Company of Birmingham would build five high-speed diesel multiple-unit sets to be introduced in 1958 on the London Midland region between London St Pancras and Manchester Central, and on the Western Region between London Paddington and Bristol and Birmingham.

At that time the design of these luxurious trains was fairly ground-breaking – the classic Pullman livery of brown and cream was replaced by blue (known as Nanking blue!) and white with a grey roof; the passenger coaches were fitted with double glazing, air conditioning and sumptuous seating and passengers were served at their tables by staff dressed in matching blue uniforms. Sporting the Pullman Car Company's crest on the nose the streamlined power cars at each end of the train were each fitted with 1,000hp NBL/MAN diesel engine driving electric transmission with a top speed of 90mph. The two LMR sets were six-car formation (this included the two non-accommodating power cars) providing 132 first class seats. The three WR sets were an eight-car formation providing 108 first class and 120 second class seats.

Following delays caused by extended trials and modifications the first Blue Pullmans entered revenue-earning service on the LMR between St Pancras and Manchester on July 4, 1960. Designed to cater for businessmen, the up service left Manchester Central during weekdays at 8.50am and, after calling at Cheadle Heath, completed the 189 mile journey to St Pancras in 193 minutes. Leaving St Pancras at 6.10pm

the return journey was completed in 191 minutes. A shorter fill-in turn from St Pancras to Nottingham and back was short lived. Following the completion of electrification between Euston and Manchester Piccadilly the two LMR sets were transferred to the Western Region in March 1967.

Blue Pullman services on the Western Region between Paddington and Bristol and Paddington and Wolverhampton Low Level commenced on September 12, 1960. An additional service was introduced between Paddington and Swansea in the summer of 1961. A steam hauled set of traditional brown and cream Pullman cars was always kept in reserve at Old Oak Common. The transfer of the two six-car sets from the LMR

in March 1967 saw the introduction of an additional service to Bristol and a new service to Oxford. The introduction of High Speed Trains on the Western Region led to the demise of Blue Pullman services, with the last train (an enthusiasts' special) running on May 5, 1973. None have been preserved.

Flying Bananas
The GWR's streamlined railcars

The GWR were never slow in keeping up with the latest trends, and their publicity department often put other railway companies to shame. The introduction of their first streamlined diesel railcar in 1933 was no exception to this; its initial success led to a total of 38 being built by 1942, their streamlined shape and their brown and cream livery giving them the nickname 'Flying Banana'. Powered by AEC diesel engines similar to those used in a London bus, they were built in three batches by Park Royal, Gloucester Railway Carriage & Wagon Company and by the GWR at Swindon. Apart from No. 1 (which only had one engine), all of the other units were fitted with twin engines. Various versions were built, including some with a small buffet section, parcels cars and two twin-sets with buffet and lavatory for longer cross-country journeys – the latter were capable of running back to back or with a single ordinary carriage between them.

When used on loss-making branch lines the introduction of the single railcars led to a steady increase in passengers, and twin-set railcars transformed services on the Cardiff to Birmingham Snow Hill (via Gloucester) route to such an extent that longer steam-hauled trains had to be introduced to cater for the extra passengers. The latter units were later transferred to the Bristol to Weymouth and Reading to Newbury routes. All but one railcar (No. 9 was destroyed in a fire in 1946) passed into British Railways ownership in 1948. Withdrawal started in 1954 with the last examples surviving until 1962. W4W, W20W and W22W have since been preserved.

Goods in Transit

British Railways freight facilities 1963

For over 100 years Britain's railways had kept the wheels of industry moving, but by the 1960s the writing was on the wall for the conveyance of individual loads by train. By 1963 the end was in sight for personalised freight services. but those that were still being advertised are now difficult to comprehend on today's 'modern' railways with their containerised trainload policy.

So cast your mind back a mere 47 years when British Railways offered an amazing choice of freight train facilities. Here are a few examples:

Express Freight Services: In addition to providing next-day delivery on overnight services between London and principal provincial stations, and also between the main provincial centres, BR ran seasonal express trains for fruit, vegetables and other kinds of market produce such as fish.

Carriage of Perishable Goods: Insulated vans and containers specially constructed for the conveyance, under refrigerated conditions, of frozen foodstuffs, quick-frozen commodities and ice-cream were available.

Farm Removals: BR undertook to transfer complete farms, including implements, livestock, etc., from one part of the country to another. Special arrangements could be made to enable cows to travel between milking times or, where very long journeys were involved, for them to be milked en route, and all animals to be fed and watered.

Works Removals: BR undertook complete works removals, including dismantling plant, etc., and its re-erection in the new works. No job was too large and all-in quotations could be given.

Packaging: In association with BR, Collico Ltd hired out collapsible cases for rail transport. The carriage charged is on net weight of contents only, the empty case is returned free.

For fuller information of any of the above ask your local goods agent or stationmaster for a copy of 'Freight Train Facilities and Services'.

LMS Famous Trains

The Royal Scot

One of the most famous long-distance expresses in the world, 'The Royal Scot' was first introduced by the London & North Western Railway and the Caledonian Railway in 1862. Departing at 10am from London Euston the train travelled the length of the West Coast Main Line to Glasgow, a distance of 401¼ miles. Hauled by one of the L&NWR's crack express locomotives such as the 4-4-0 Precursor or the later 4-6-0 Claughton, the train required banking assistance on the climb to Shap before arriving at Carlisle where a Caledonian Railway loco took over.

Following the 'Big Four' Railway Grouping of 1923 'The Royal Scot' became the premier express train of the LMS and the introduction of the Fowler-designed 7P 'Royal Scot' Class 4-6-0s in 1927 led to a greatly improved service with heavier loadings. However, even these powerful locos still needed assistance over Shap – a situation which was only remedied in 1933 with the introduction of Stanier's 8P 'Princess Royal' Class Pacifics. By then the train had officially become non-stop but in reality it still stopped at Carlisle for a crew change. 'Coronation' Class Pacifics took over in 1937, a duty they were to retain until the end of steam haulage in the early 1960s. By 1962 the departure from Euston had been re-timed to 9.30am and, with a stop at Carlisle, the train reached Glasgow at 4.50pm (Monday–Friday). The Saturday working took

40 minutes longer and on Sundays the train was virtually reduced to stopping-train status with stops at Rugby, Crewe, Carlisle, Beattock and Motherwell, arriving at Glasgow at 7.20pm.

Following electrification of the WCML to Glasgow in 1974 'The Royal Scot' continued to run until 2003 when the name was dropped. Existing Pendolino Class 390 trains from Euston to Glasgow now take only 4hr 31min to complete the journey.

THE THAMES-CLYDE EXPRESS

The alternative and more scenic route from London to Glasgow was via the ex-Midland Railway line from St Pancras to Carlisle via Leeds and the Settle & Carlisle line, and then to Glasgow St Enoch via Dumfries over ex-G&SWR metals. In 1927 the LMS gave the name 'Thames-Clyde Express' to its 10am departure from St Pancras to Glasgow St Enoch and the 9.30am departure in the opposite direction. Although serving major population centres in the East Midlands and Yorkshire the route was much longer and steeper than the alternative WCML, consequently the journey was much longer. Suspended during World War II the 'Thames-Clyde Express' was restored in 1949. During this post-war period the train was usually headed by either 'Jubilee' or 'Royal Scot' 4-6-0s until these were replaced by BR Sulzer Type 4 diesels. Journey times remained poor – the summer 1962 timetable showed the train departing St Pancras at 10.10am and, after calling at Leicester, Chesterfield, Sheffield, Leeds, Carlisle, Annan, Dumfries and Kilmarnock, arrived at St Enoch at 7.50pm, a journey time of 9hr 40min – 2hr 20min slower than the rival 'Royal Scot'. This couldn't go on much longer, and with the completion of WCML electrification in 1974 the train lost its title.

Welsh Phoenix

The re-birth of the Welsh Highland Railway

What must be one of the most complicated stories of the life of a railway has recently been completed with the re-opening of the Welsh Highland Railway between Caernarfon and Porthmadog in North Wales.

In the beginning was the North Wales Narrow Gauge Railways Company's (NWNGR) 1ft 11½in-gauge line, which opened between Dinas Junction, south of Caernarfon, and slate quarries at Bryngwyn in 1877. A branch to Rhyd-Ddu, on the lower western slopes of Snowdon, was opened in 1881. Despite financial problems the NWNGR acquired a Light Railway Order in 1900 to extend southwards from Rhyd-Ddu to

Beddgelert, but this was never built. Another company, the long-winded Portmadoc, Beddgelert & South Snowdon Railway (PBSSR), started construction of a line northwards from Croesor Junction, on the antiquated Croesor Tramway, to link with the NWNGR's southern terminus via Beddgelert. Although some earthworks were built, the project was soon abandoned.

The next twist in this tale came in 1921 when, with the financial backing from the Government and local authorities, the Welsh Highland Railway was formed by taking over the NWNGR and what remained

of the PBSSR. The missing link between Rhyd-Ddu and Croesor Junction and the re-laid Croesor Tramway to Porthmadog was opened in 1923. With borrowed locomotives and rolling stock from the Ffestiniog Railway the new company struggled on until 1934 when the Ffestiniog agreed to lease the line. Despite the latter's efforts to make the line a success it was short-lived, and all trains ceased to run in 1937. The line was finally lifted in 1941 and the trackbed, owned by Caernarvonshire County Council, slowly reverted to nature.

Fast forward to 2009, following 45 years of legal wranglings, volunteer effort and major funding from the Millennium Commission, European Regional Development Board, the Welsh Assembly and the Wales Tourist Board – the Welsh Highland Railway has risen like a phoenix from the ashes. Hauled by narrow gauge Beyer-Garratt locos rescued from South Africa, trains now run from Caernarfon along the route of the closed standard gauge line to Dinas and then south to Porthmadog via Beddgelert and the beautiful Aberglaslyn Pass. At Porthmadog passengers can continue their journey to Blaenau Ffestiniog on the Ffestiniog Railway, making the 40-mile journey from Caernarfon the longest narrow gauge ride in Britain.

Snoring Along the Line
The rise and fall of the sleeping car train

The first sleeping car in Britain was introduced by the North British Railway on 2 April, 1873 between London King's Cross and Glasgow Queen Street. Other companies were soon following suit by using Pullman cars with convertible seating. All sleeping arrangements on trains were communal until the GWR introduced a sleeping car with double berth cabins, similar to those still used today, in 1890.

By the turn of the century sleeping car trains were running from London to Scotland, the West Country, North Wales and northern England. These services remained fairly intact until the 1960s, by which time British Rail were running around 40 trains on most nights.

Apart from the cross-Channel services to Paris and Brussels on 'The Night Ferry' there were no sleeping car trains on the Southern Region. The Western Region ran services from Paddington to Birkenhead Woodside, Carmarthen, Penzance, Plymouth and between Plymouth and Manchester.

With the advent of cheaper domestic air travel and high-speed motorways BR's network of sleeping car trains has shrunk considerably since the heady days of the 1960s. Now only two routes remain in operation, the 'Caledonian Sleeper' and the

'Night Riviera,' and even the long-term future of these remain in doubt. Operating six nights each week, these trains are among the last locomotive-hauled passenger trains in the UK.

'CALEDONIAN SLEEPER'

This is effectively two trains – the Lowland Caledonian Sleeper carries two portions between London Euston and Glasgow/ Edinburgh. The Highland Caledonian Sleeper carries three portions between Euston and Aberdeen/Inverness/Fort William.

LMR TIMETABLE FOR 1961

LONDON TO:

Barrow-in-Furness
Carlisle
Corkikle
Edinburgh Waverley
Galashiels
Glasgow Central
Glasgow St Enoch
Holyhead
Inverness
Aberdeen (w)
Arbroath (w)
Dundee (w)
Edinburgh Waverley (w)
Fort William (w)
Montrose (w)
Newcastle (w)
Leeds City
Liverpool Lime Street
Manchester Piccadilly
Motherwell
Oban
Perth
Preston
Stranraer Harbour

BIRMINGHAM TO:

Glasgow
Newcastle
Bristol
Edinburgh Princes Street

GLASGOW TO:

Liverpool
Manchester
Plymouth

All at Sea

Railway-owned docks, harbours and ships

As an island nation Britain depends on foreign trade for its survival – the majority of our imports and exports still go by sea. The coming of the industrial age and the building of railways during the 19th century saw a vast expansion of trade, and by the beginning of the 20th century the power of Britain's railways had extended over the sea as well as over land. By that time, although no shipping company owned a railway, a great many railway companies owned ships, and an even larger number owned docks and harbours. Here are some of the marine undertakings:

London & North Western Railway: Holyhead Harbour, Greenore Harbour (Ireland), Garston Docks near Liverpool, joint owner with Lancashire & Yorkshire Railway of Fleetwood Docks; 16 steamships and joint ownership of eight other steamships.

Great Western Railway: harbours at Plymouth, Llanelly, Briton Ferry, Brentford, Bridgwater, Newquay and New Milford and joint ownership of Fishguard Harbour and Rosslare Harbour in Ireland; 16 steamships.

North Eastern Railway: docks at Hull, Hartlepoool, Tyne Dock (exporting 7 million tons of coal per annum), Middlesbrough, Monkwearmouth and coal staithes at Blyth and Dunston-on-the-Tyne.

Midland Railway: harbour at Heysham and four steamships for Isle of Man service.

Great Central Railway: docks at Grimsby and 13 steamships for North Sea trade.

Lancashire & Yorkshire Railway: docks at Fleetwood, five steamships and joint owner of five other steamships. Owned Goole Shipping Company.

Great Eastern Railway: harbour at Parkeston Quay and 12 steamships.

London & South Western Railway: Southampton Docks and 15 steamships.

London Brighton & South Coast Railway: Newhaven Harbour, two steamships and joint owner of 14 steamships, Isle of Wight ferries.

South-Eastern & Chatham Railway: harbours at Folkestone and Whitstable and facilities at Port Victoria, Queenborough, Strood, Gravesend, Rye and Dover, joint owner of 19 steamships.

Taff Vale Railway: Penarth Docks and Harbour, exporting four million tons of coal per annum.

Barry Railway: Barry Docks, exporting nine million tons of coal per annum.

Cardiff Railway: Bute Docks.

North British Railway: docks at Methil, Burntisland, Bo'ness, Alloa, Charlestown, Kincardine, Tayport, Silloth and Mallaig, and seven steamships.

Glasgow & South Western Railway: harbours at Troon, Largs and Fairlie and ten steamships.

Trains don't Run Here Anymore

Lost railway journeys on the Western and Southern Regions of BR

Until the closure of thousands of miles of railway lines in the 1950s and '60s, it was still possible to travel from almost anywhere to anywhere else throughout Britain. Thanks mainly to Dr Beeching and his political paymasters, many of these journeys by rail are no longer possible but our intrepid armchair traveller can still sit and dream of what was once possible. Dipping at random into old British Railways' regional timetables, here are a few gems that are gone forever.

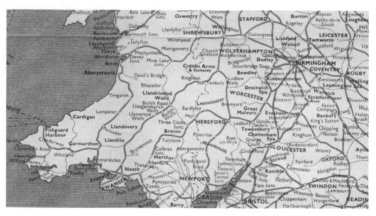

A journey from Cardigan to Stratford-upon-Avon involved 209¼ miles of mainly branch line and secondary routes involving eight changes of train at Whitland, Carmarthen, Llandilo, Builth Road, Three Cocks Junction, Hereford, Gloucester and Cheltenham! The journey started at Cardigan at 10am, and arrived at Stratford-upon-Avon at 10.24pm – and all hauled by steam! Apart from two short sections, between Whitland and Carmarthen and Gloucester to Cheltenham, the entire journey is no longer possible.

SOUTHERN REGION
WEEKDAYS, SUMMER 1963

LYME REGIS TO PADSTOW
(VIA THE LONG WAY ROUND)

Itinerary

Lyme Regis	dep. 8.14am
Axminster	arr. 8.32am
Axminster	dep. 8.35am
Sidmouth Junction	arr. 9.03am
Sidmouth Junction	dep. 9.28am
Tipton St John's	arr. 9.39am
Tipton St John's	dep. 9.47am
Exmouth	arr. 10.19am
Exmouth	dep. 10.44am
Exeter (Central)	arr. 11.10am
Exeter (Central)	dep. 11.27am
Ilfracombe	arr. 1.44pm
Ilfracombe	dep. 2.20pm
Barnstaple Junction	arr. 2.58pm
Barnstaple Junction	dep. 3.18pm
Torrington	arr. 3.49pm
Torrington	dep. 4.00pm
Halwill Junction	arr. 5.23pm
Halwill Junction	dep. 6.22pm
Wadebridge	arr. 7.48pm
Wadebridge	dep. 8.42pm
Padstow	arr. 8.52pm

By this date all lines west of Salisbury were in the hands of the dreaded Western Region but, for old times sake, we take a complicated steam-hauled journey along many ex-SR highways and byways that were soon to close. The 202.5 miles of railway, involving no less than ten changes, are now a fading memory.

The 2nd Beeching Report

The little-known proposed destruction of Britain's railways

We have all heard of Dr Beeching's report 'The Reshaping of British Railways' which was published in March 1963, and we all know that one part of its recommendations, the wholesale closure of cross-country and branch lines, was eagerly implemented by both the outgoing Conservative government and the new Labour government under Harold Wilson. Although a few lines, such as the Far North of Scotland, Ayr to Stranraer, Settle & Carlisle, Cumbrian Coast, and Central Wales, eventually escaped the axe, over 4,000 miles were closed by 1966, leaving vast swathes of the country with no access to rail services. A further 2,000 miles had gone by the end of the decade, even though Labour had made an election pledge in 1964 to halt the closures.

What is less well-known is that Dr Beeching, the first chairman of the British Railways Board, also published a second report early in 1965 entitled 'The Development of the Major Railway Trunk Routes'. In this report he proposed investment in just nine main lines serving only major centres of population and industry. By implication there would have been further swingeing closures of another 4,500 miles of railway, but this time they weren't just branch lines or lightly used cross-country routes but, in many cases, major trunk routes. It seems inconceivable now that they would even have been considered, but the following closures were proposed:

Perth to Inverness, Aberdeen to Inverness, the ex-G&SWR line from Carlisle to Glasgow, all lines west and southwest of Glasgow, the ECML north of Newcastle, all lines to Scarborough, Leeds to Carnforth and Barrow, all railways in Wales apart from the main Newport, Cardiff and Swansea corridor, the Midland main line, all lines in East Anglia apart from Liverpool St to Norwich, all lines in north Kent, London to Hastings and the South Coast route through Eastbourne, Bath to Southampton via Westbury, the ex-GWR route from Reading to Taunton via Westbury, the former L&SWR main line west from Basingstoke to Exeter, all routes to Weymouth and, finally, all railway lines west of Plymouth.

Even this was too much to stomach for the new Labour government who promptly rejected the report. Three months after it was published Dr Beeching resigned as Chairman of the British Railways Board and returned to his old job with ICI – in fact it was rumoured that he was sacked by the then Minister of Transport, Tom Fraser. Needless to say Dr Beeching was still rewarded in the 1965 Birthday Honours and made a life peer!

Locomotive Builders to the British Empire

The story of Beyer-Peacock

The locomotive building company Beyer-Peacock was founded in 1853 by English engineer Richard Peacock, German-born Charles Beyer and Scottish engineer Henry Robertson. With its extensive works at Gorton Foundry, Manchester the company went on to build 4,753 tender locos and 1,735 tank locos for countries ranging from India, Sweden, Spain, Egypt, Turkey, Belgium, Holland, Germany and Italy to Peru, Brazil, Uruguay, Dutch East Indies and the Australian states, as well as for many British railway companies. They also built 1,115 Beyer-Garratt articulated locos between 1909 and 1958 for Australia, India, Brazil, Burma, Chile, Ecuador, Brazil, Russia, New Zealand, Sierra Leone, South Africa, Kenya, Uganda, Rhodesia, Nigeria, Iran, Sudan, Angola and last, but not least, the LMS and the LNER in Britain. Of note was the largest steam engine built in Europe – with a tractive effort of 90,000lb the 4-8-2+2-8-4 Garratt was supplied to Russian Railways in 1932 – and the world's most powerful

narrow gauge locos – the 3ft 6in gauge Garratts supplied to South African Railways in 1929. During World War II the company produced tanks and shells alongside continuing loco production – a Garratt for Burma Railways was designed and built in a record time of 118 days!

By 1958 steam engine production was at an end, but Beyer-Peacock went on to build electric and diesel main line locos for BR. This changeover to modern traction proved uneconomic for Beyer-Peacock, and the company was forced to close in 1966. Happily, many preserved examples can still be seen in operation around the world.

DIESEL MAIN LINE LOCOMOTIVES BUILT BY BEYER-PEACOCK FOR BR

101 Hymek B-B diesel hydraulics D7000-D7100 (Class 35) 1961–1964
These strikingly designed diesels were built for the Western Region but their non-standard transmission had led to their demise by 1975.

62 Sulzer Type 2 Bo-Bo diesel electric D7598-D7660 (Class 25/3) in 1966
These fairly successful maids-of-all-work had all been withdrawn by 1987.

29 Clayton Type 1 Bo-Bo diesel electric D8588-D8616 (Class 17) 1964–65
Not a successful type and the whole class had been withdrawn by 1971.

10 Class 82 Bo-Bo electric locos E3046-E3055 for WCML 1960–1962
Two of the class were destroyed in fires while the remainder were rebuilt in the 1970s. The last two examples were withdrawn in 1987.

On Shed, March 29, 1964

An almighty shed bash around Glasgow and Edinburgh

Spurred on by the imminent end to steam haulage on BR, many railway societies, including the Warwickshire Railway Society and the Home Counties Railway Society, organised trips during the early 1960s to distant engine sheds and railway works for their members. Known as 'shed bashes', many of these trips had to be undertaken by road coach due to the difficulties in organising an itinerary, usually on a Sunday, that took in obscure destinations that had long lost their passenger service. Fortunately, not all of these trips were made by road and one of them, organised by (I believe) the Warwickshire Railway Society for March 28–30, 1964, was a shed bash to end all shed bashes!

On the evening of March 28 hundreds of fellow trainspotters and I gathered in the gloomy depths of Birmingham New Street station to await the arrival of our special to Glasgow and Edinburgh. By that date the diesel invasion was well underway and my trip up from Gloucester on a Bristol to Newcastle train that evening had been behind BR Sulzer Type 4 D35. However, I was not to be disappointed when our special train drew into New Street behind gleaming maroon-liveried 'Coronation' Class 4-6-2 No. 46256 'Sir William A. Stanier, F.R.S.' – with only six months to go before withdrawal this powerful machine was much in demand for specials such as ours. Departure from New Street was prompt at 11pm and with pick-ups at Crewe (12.35am) and Preston (1.47am) we arrived at Glasgow Central at 6.20am on the 29th.

There must have been around 400 trainspotters who alighted bleary eyed from that train, and in a monumental exercise that would have done justice to the British Army we were transported in a fleet of coaches to ten engine sheds around the Glasgow and Edinburgh area. From early morning until early evening this vast army with notebooks and cameras to hand visited engine sheds at Polmadie (66A), Motherwell (66B), Corkerhill (67A), Dawsholm (65D), Eastfield (65A), St Rollox (65B), Bathgate (64F), Haymarket (64B), Dalry Road (64C), and St Margarets (64A). At the end of that day we were dumped on Waverley station to wait for our train to take us back to Birmingham. Departure from Waverley was at 10.35pm and there were drop-offs at Preston (3.20am) and Crewe (4.34am) – however I must have fallen asleep soon after departure as I cannot remember much of the journey back (I suppose we must have travelled back via the Waverley Route). 'Sir William' came off at Crewe where 'Black Five' 4-6-0 No. 44765 took over for the rest of the journey to New Street, where we arrived at 6.08am on the 30th. Weary and exhausted after spotting a total of 675 locos (353 steam, 313 diesel, 9 electric), I snoozed on the way back to Gloucester behind BR Sulzer Type 4 D126. What a trip!

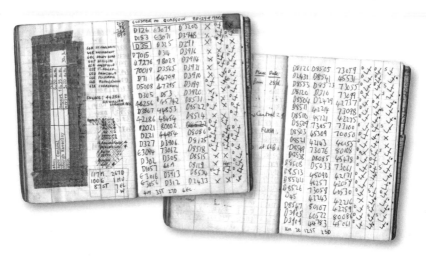

Raised From The Dead

The story of Dai Woodham's Barry scrapyard

The 1960s were a boom period for scrapyards up and down the country – the BR Modernisation Plan of 1955 spelt the end for 16,000 steam locomotives, 16,000 carriages and 625,000 goods wagons. These all had to be disposed of and by the end of the 1950s the various railway works around the country were already full to bursting with withdrawn locos, carriages and wagons. Enter scrap metal merchant Dai Woodham, who became the first recipient of withdrawn Western Region locos and wagons from Swindon at his Barry scrapyard.

The first engines sent to Barry – four Moguls and a Prairie tank – arrived in March 1959, and within a few years this slow trickle became a torrent, not only of steam locomotives but also of thousands of wooden goods wagons and brake vans. Soon the scrapping of the steam locomotives was put on the back burner so that Woodham's could concentrate on disposing of the backlog of goods wagons – by 1968, 297 locos had been sold to the company but they had only scrapped 80. The picture was very different at other scrapyards around the country where withdrawn locos were disposed of fairly quickly.

By 1968 the railway preservation movement was gaining momentum

> **DID YOU KNOW?**
>
> BR initially insisted that the engines be removed from Woodham's yard by one of their diesels, with a braking van to provide additional support. In 1976 BR decided that all locomotives had to be transported by road to the M4.

and Woodham's was the only source of steam engines – albeit many of them by now rusting hulks. Many of them lay at Barry for over 20 years, with the longest resident being ex-GWR 2-6-2 tank No. 5552 which arrived in May 1961 and was liberated in June 1986 – over 25 years on 'death row'. Western Region locos saved include 11 'Hall', five 'Castle', two 'King', six 'Modified Hall' and eight 'Manor' 4-6-0s. Representatives of the Southern Region, particularly Bulleid Pacifics, fared even better as most of them were withdrawn towards the end of steam on BR and include 10 'West Country', eight 'Battle of Britain' and 10 'Merchant Navy' Pacifics. 45 ex-LMS locos were also saved including two 'Jubilees', six 'Black Fives' and six '8Fs'. Even two Somerset & Dorset Joint Railway 7F 2-8-0s and the unique BR 8P Pacific No. 71000 'Duke of Gloucester' were saved for posterity. Oddly, only one ex-LNER loco, 'B1' 4-6-0 No. 61264, was bought by Dai Woodham and, after spending nearly eight years there was also saved for preservation.

Steam locos saved from Barry:
38 BR Standard locos
98 ex-GWR locos
41 ex-SR locos
35 ex-LMS locos
1 ex-LNER loco

The site of Barry scrapyard has now been completely cleared and all traces of this important resting place for Britain's steam locomotives have been erased.

The Slow & Dirty

A journey over the S&DJR in 1963

SOUTHERN RAILWAY (South Western Section).
787
FROM WATERLOO TO
WINCANTON

By 1963 through passenger trains from the North and the Midlands to Bournemouth via the Somerset & Dorset Joint Railway had ceased, and customers wishing to avail themselves of this route were subjected to a reduced stopping train service between Bath Green Park and Bournemouth West. The die had already been cast for the line's closure in 1966.

As a young lad I was lucky that my father didn't own a car so the train journey from our hometown of Gloucester to our annual holiday destination was pure joy. To my mother's concern I usually spent most of the journey with my head out of the window taking down loco numbers.

The annual holiday in 1963 was in Lyme Regis and I not only wrote down numbers of locos seen but also kept a meticulous

record of the journey taken on August via Mangotsfield, Bath Green Park, Templecombe and Axminster. On the opposite page is the unabridged and unexpurgated record of that journey. Those were the days!

'We left Gloucester Eastgate on an overcast morning at 7.30. No. 73068 pulled us with only three coaches. Stopped at all stations except Haresfield. By the time we left Yate the train was full of people. On the way I observed 5420 at Berkeley Road on a Sharpness train and also a 'Hall' on an up South Wales relief train which crossed over our line at Yate. A top speed of 62mph was recorded between Berkeley Road and Charfield. We arrived at Mangotsfield on time and then had to wait an hour for our connection to Templecombe. Whilst I waited there I observed No. 44776 roaring through on a Bristol to Newcastle extra. Our train consisted of six coaches, three of which were in Southern green, and was pulled by 2-6-2T No. 41249 as far as Bath (Green Park). On passing Bath engine shed I saw S&D 2-8-0 No. 53808 and a couple of WR pannier tanks. The engine which was going to pull us to Templecombe was No. 73054, which backed onto our train and we left Bath ten minutes late. We climbed steadily but slowly up the gradient to Midford, passing through several smoky single line tunnels. The journey to Templecombe was uneventful; we passed only two trains on the way there, one of which was a goods hauled by a S&D 2-8-0. By the time we reached Templecombe it was raining steadily and as we passed the engine shed I noted quite a few engines, among them S&D 2-87-0 No. 53809, two 32XX 0-6-0, standard tanks and No. 75053. We pulled into Templecombe fifteen minutes late and our train from Waterloo soon arrived behind Merchant Navy No. 35016 (Elders Fyffes). The engines seen on the way to Axminster were two unrebuilt and two rebuilt light Pacifics, U1 2-6-0, S15, and No. 4593 on a Yeovil Town to Yeovil Junction push-pull. We reached a maximum speed of 87mph between Templecombe and Yeovil Junction and arrived at Axminster five minutes late. Our train to Lyme Regis was already waiting behind Ivatt 2-6-2T No. 41307. We reached Lyme Regis exactly at one o'clock.'

Behind the Scenes

British Railways' motley collection of departmental and service locomotives

By 1961 the writing was on the wall for British Railways' large fleet of steam locomotives. The diesel invasion was underway and mass withdrawals of steam locos were taking place – however there were a few hidden corners of this vast empire where veteran steam, diesel and electric locomotives were still hard at work. Never seen in regular service they trundled around railway works, engineers' departments, sleeper depots or railway-owned quarries and were classed as Departmental or Service

Locomotives – what a motley crew they were!

Of all the BR regions the Western was the most up-to-date, making use of pretty standard fare such as pannier tanks around Swindon Works and a small collection of 1950s diesel service locos – the total tally was 0-4-0 No. 20, 0-6-0s PWM650, PWM654 and two petrol locomotives Nos. 24 and 27.

The Southern Region had a more mixed bag including two 0-4-0 diesel locos Nos. DS600 and DS1169 (Broad Clyst) and 0-6-0 No. DS1173 (Engineer's Dept). There were two electric locos – DS74 (Durnsford Road power station) and DS75 (Waterloo & City line). The steam bag consisted of ex LB&SCR/SE&CR A1 Class 0-6-0s DS680 and DS681 and ex-LB&SCR A1X Class 0-6-0 DS681 (all three at Lancing Carriage Works)

and ex-L&SWR G6 0-6-0s DS682 (30238) and DS3152 (30272) – the last two working at Meldon Quarry.

The London Midland Region had seven 0-4-0 standard gauge service diesels (ED1-ED7) all built by John Fowler in 1936 except ED7 which was built in 1955. ED10 was a 3ft gauge diesel built by Ruston & Hornsby in 1955 for working at Beeston (Notts) Sleeper Depot – the loco is preserved at the Irchester Narrow Gauge Railway Trust. The ex-L&YR works at Horwich still had an 18in gauge system in 1961 that was operated by 1887-vintage 0-4-0 saddle tank 'Wren' (now part of the National Collection) and 0-4-0 diesel ZM32 (built by Ruston & Hornsby in 1957 and now preserved at the Steeple Grange Light Railway). Still carrying their LMS numbers were ex-L&YR standard gauge 0-6-0 2F saddle tanks Nos 11304, 11305, 11324 and 11368. Other LMR steam locos carrying their BR numbering including 'Jinty' 3F 0-6-0T, ex-L&YR 2F 0-6-0ST and 3F 0-6-0T were used as service locos at Horwich, Crewe and Wolverton Works.

The Eastern and North Eastern Regions probably had the most interesting collection of departmental locomotives. Apart from 1950s-built diesel shunters (0-4-0 Nos 52, 56, 81 and 85 and 0-6-0 Nos 88, 91 and 92) and Bo-Bo electric loco No. 100 the rest were a very mixed bag of steam locos – Nos. 2 and 9 were ex-GNR Class J52/2 0-6-0 saddle tanks, Nos. 7, 40 and 41 were Class Y3 0-4-0 geared Sentinel tanks, No. 32 was an ex-GER Class J66 0-6-0 tank, Nos. 44 and 45 were ex-GER Class J69 0-6-0 tanks, Nos. 39 and 54 were Class Y1 0-4-0 geared Sentinel tanks and No. 33 was an ex-GER Class Y4 0-4-0 tank.

Night Mail
The story of the travelling Post Office

Mail was first carried by train on the Liverpool & Manchester Railway in 1830. Soon, the vast increase in the amount of mail led to ways of devising a sorting system on board the train. A converted horse-box with three mail sorters, the first Travelling Post Office (TPO) ran in January 1838 on the Grand Junction Railway between Birmingham and Warrington. This was so successful that it gave rise to the Railways (Conveyance of Mails) Act later that year, in which all railway companies were required to carry mail.

The introduction of Rowland Hill's uniform Penny Post system in 1840 led to a further upsurge in business, and a growth in TPOs throughout the country. By 1852 there were 39 sorting clerks employed on services as far north as Perth and as far south as Exeter. The service was so successful that by 1885 specially-dedicated mail trains,

DID YOU KNOW?
By the outbreak of World War I there were over 130 TPO services across the country, although this number was never achieved again.

with no passenger accommodation, were introduced. Suspended during both World Wars, the TPO saw its routes much reduced until only 43 remained when services were reintroduced in 1945. From then on it was

downhill all the way – by 1988 there were 35 TPOs and in 1994 there were only 24 – and on the night of January 9, 2004, the last remaining services made their final journey.

Lineside apparatus to pick up and drop down mail while travelling at speed was first introduced in 1838 on the London & Birmingham Railway at Berkhamsted and Leighton Buzzard (site of the 1963 Great Train Robbery). An improved version with moveable nets fixed to the train and at the lineside came into operation in 1848 – this system remained in use in 1971.

'Night Mail'

'This is the Night Mail crossing the border
Bringing the cheque and the postal order...'

One of the most famous documentary films ever made, *Night Mail* starred the West Coast Postal Special TPO, its crew and 'Royal Scot' 4-6-0 No. 6115 'Scots Guardsman' on their overnight journey from London to Glasgow. Made by the General Post Office Film Unit in 1936, this classic short film features music by Benjamin Britten and verse by W H Auden.

Prepare for Take-off

Britain's railway-owned airline

Even back in the late 1920s the railways saw domestic airlines as a serious threat, so in 1929 the 'Big Four' – GWR, LMS, LNER and SR – obtained Parliamentary approval to run their own air services. Apart from SR's unsuccessful attempt to take control of Imperial Airways, nothing much happened until 1933 when the GWR started an air service for mail and passengers linking Cardiff and Plymouth – an obvious choice as the meandering rail journey via Bristol was 164¾ miles, while the direct air route across the Bristol Channel was around 90 miles. Birmingham, Teignmouth and Torquay were also soon added to the GWR's network.

In March 1934 the 'Big Four' railway companies and Imperial Airways formed Railway Air Services Ltd (RAS) – the first chairman of RAS was Sir Harold Hartley of the LMS and the first flight was by a de Haviland Dragon on the Plymouth-Haldon-Cardiff-Birmingham route. The RAS network soon expanded to include Croydon, Brighton & Hove, Portsmouth, Isle of Wight, Southampton, Bournemouth, Exeter, Plymouth, Bristol, Cardiff, Cheltenham & Gloucester, Birmingham, Stoke-on-Trent, Manchester, Liverpool, Belfast and Glasgow using de Haviland Dragon and Dragon Rapide and Express 'airliners'.

Apart from the Liverpool-Belfast-Glasgow route the airline ceased operations during World War II, but resumed in 1946 with Avro Ansons and DC3s. RAS was taken over by the newly-formed state-owned British European Airways in 1947.

Locomotive Builder to the British Empire

The story of the North British Locomotive Company

> **DID YOU KNOW?**
>
> NBL also built ten Class AL4 Bo-Bo electric locos (E3036-E3045) in 1960-61 for the WCML. Even these were unreliable and, despite rebuilding in the early '70s, they had all been withdrawn by 1980.

Formed in 1903 by the merger of three Glasgow locomotive manufacturers (Dübs, Neilson and Sharp Stewart) the North British Locomotive Company (NBL) became the largest locomotive manufacturer in Europe with a capacity to build 600 per year. With its headquarters in Springburn in the north of the city, the NBL went on until the mid-1950s to build thousands of steam locos, not only for British companies such as the SR and LMS, but also for the War Department in World War II, and railways in Australia, New Zealand, Malaysia, Pakistan, India and South Africa. Some of these locos have since been preserved and are still in steam.

NOTABLE BRITISH STEAM LOCOS BUILT BY NBL

Southern Railway: 30 'King Arthur' Class 4-6-0 (763-792) in 192.

London Midland & Scottish Railway: 25 Compound 4P 4-4-0, 50 'Royal Scot' 4-6-0s (6100-6149) in 1927, 50 'Jubilee' Class 4-6-0 (5557-5606) in 1934–35.

War Department: 208 Stanier 8F 2-8-0, 150 8F 2-10-0 and 545 8F 2-8-0 in 1943.

Sadly the NBL failed to continue its long and illustrious record when it moved from steam to diesel production in the late 1950s. After signing a deal with the German company MAN to build diesel engines under licence it went on to build some of the most unreliable locomotives ever ordered by BR, and the taxpayer footed the bill.

The poor workmanship and unreliability of NBL locos brought the company to its knees. Warranty claims and guarantees finally pushed the company over the brink and it went bankrupt in April 1962. All that remains today are the company's former offices in Flemington Street, Springburn which are now part of the North Glasgow College.

NBL DIESEL FAILURES

58 Type 2 Bo-Bo diesel electric (Class 21) D6100-D6157 1958-60
Apart from 20 which were rebuilt as Class 29, all had been withdrawn by 1968. The Class 29 faired little better and were withdrawn by 1971.

58 Type 2 B-B diesel hydraulic (Class 22) D6300-D6357 1959-1962
The class had become extinct by 1972.

5 Type 4 A1A-A1A diesel hydraulic (Class 41) D600-D604 1958-59
All withdrawn at end of 1967.

33 Type 4 B-B diesel hydraulic (Class 43) D833-D865 1960-1962
All withdrawn by 1971.

LNER Famous Trains
The Flying Scotsman

By 1860 services on the East Coast Main Line (ECML) between London King's Cross and Edinburgh Waverley were under the control of the Great Northern Railway, the North Eastern Railway and the North British Railway. Through services between the two capitals were hindered by the lack of standard passenger carriages and in that year the three companies formed the East Coast Joint Stock to remedy this situation.

By 1862 new rolling stock for the first 'Special Scotch Express' was ready, and the train became a regular feature departing each day at 10am from King's Cross and Waverley stations. At that time the train took a leisurely 10½ hours to complete the 393 miles, including a disembarkation for passengers at York for a spot of lunch. This leisurely pace wasn't to last long, and when Patrick Stirling, the GNR's Chief Mechanical Engineer, designed his famous Stirling Single locomotives in 1870 the East Coast route saw a rapid acceleration of schedules with a whole two hours soon being lopped of the King's Cross to Edinburgh journey.

Speed limits

By 1888 there had also developed a serious rivalry between the operators of the West Coast Main Line (L&NWR and CR) and the East Coast Main Line (GNR, NER, NBR) to achieve the fastest possible time between the two capitals. This resulted in what became known as the 'Race to the North' and, on August 20 that year with the surefooted help from the Stirling Singles as far as York, the ECML between King's Cross and Edinburgh was covered in 6hr 19min at an average speed of 62.2mph. The rivalry continued until 1896 when an Anglo-Scottish express, operated by the L&NWR, was derailed at Preston – safety limits had been flouted and a speed limit was imposed on the two rivals which stayed in place until 1932.

The beginning of the 20th century brought major improvements to the 'Special Scotch Express', with modern corridor carriages and dining cars. The heavier and longer trains were now headed by Ivatt's new 'Atlantics' as far as York, but timings remained the same due to the 1896 speed restriction. The arrival of Nigel Gresley as Locomotive Engineer of the Great Northern Railway in 1911 led to the building of a series of groundbreaking 'Pacific' locomotive types. Two of his Class 'A1' were built at Doncaster in 1922, and ten more had been ordered just before the 'Big Four' Grouping of 1923. As CME of the newly-formed LNER, Gresley went on to develop this design into the 'A3' and later 'A4' streamlined Pacifics.

The naming of a legend

The 'Special Scotch Express' became officially known as the 'Flying Scotsman' in 1924, and one of Gresley's 'A1' locos, No 4472, was also named in honour of the train. To reduce the journey time between King's Cross and Edinburgh some of the 'A1' locos were fitted with larger tenders not only containing more coal, but also with a corridor linking the engine to the first coach of the train. The latter allowed a crew changeover halfway through the journey, and so in May 1928 'The Flying Scotsman' became a non-stop service, complete with a host of on-board facilities.

Full speed ahead

The speed limitation agreement was abolished in 1932 and the gloves were off – by 1938 the journey time for the down 'Flying Scotsman' had been reduced to 7hr 20min. The austerity measures of World War II soon brought an end to high-speed rail travel and it took some years before pre-War schedules were being attained. With the introduction of the record-breaking non-stop 'Elizabethan' express in 1954 (taking only 6½ hours to cover the 393 miles), the 'Flying Scotsman' had reverted to an intermediate stop at Newcastle – even though the journey time by 1961 had come down to 7hr 2min with the introduction of the new 'Deltic' (Class 55) diesels.

The introduction of 100mph-running along many stretches of the ECML gave the 'Deltics' their racing ground, and timings for 'The Flying Scotsman' continued to tumble. In turn, the 'Deltics' were replaced by HST sets between 1976 and 1981, and the opening of the Selby diversion improved matters further. Electrification was completed in 1990 and since then InterCity 125 sets with a maximum permissible speed of 125mph have provided an even faster service. Currently the 10.00am departure from King's Cross takes only 4hr 23 min to reach Edinburgh – progress indeed!

STOP PRESS

Railway news, May 1929

* A number of old L&NWR 'Renown' Class and 'George the Fifth' Class 4-4-0s and 'Prince of Wales' Class 4-6-0s bearing similar names to those allotted to some of the new 'Royal Scot' class engines will probably lose their nameplates shortly.

* 'Royal Scot' Class No. 6118 'Royal Welch Fusilier' was recently noted in the Liverpool district with the tender of No. 6115 'Scots Guardsman' attached.

* The Southern railway locomotive No. 783 'Sir Gillemere' which drew the train in which Major Segrave travelled from Southampton to London, bore the words "Welcome Home, Major Segrave".

* LNER locomotives 2755 'Berkshire', 2756 'Selkirkshire' and 2757 'Dumfriesshire' have been seen working near Glasgow.

* Six Sentinel Cammell steam railcars are now working in the Scottish area – No. 31 'Flower of Yarrow', No. 32 'Fair Maid', No. 33 'Highland Chieftain', No. 34 'Tweedside', No. 35 'Nettle' and No. 36 'Royal Eagle' have been put into service in Edinburgh, Stirling, Aberdeen and Carlisle.

* New engines that have been received from the North British Locomotive Co. Ltd., of Glasgow include 0-6-0 tank locomotives Nos. 5700-7 and Nos. 5726-9. Tank goods 2-6-2 locomotives No. 5565-9 have been turned out of Swindon Works.

* The large marshalling yard of the LNER at Whitemoor, near March, is now nearing completion. It has ten reception roads, each of which holds 80 goods wagons and a hump with a 1 in 18 descent for gravitational shunting. Wagons are sorted into four groups of sidings with each group containing ten sidings making a total accommodation of 3,679 wagons.

The Muddle & Get Nowhere Railway

The long-lamented Midland & Great Northern Joint Railway

Formed in 1862 the mighty Great Eastern Railway had a virtual stranglehold on railways in East Anglia which lasted another 31 years until the formation of the Midland & Great Northern Joint Railway in 1893. As its name suggests, the railway was jointly owned by the Great Northern Railway and the Midland Railway – the latter eager to extend its sphere of influence to the towns and ports of Norfolk, saw an opportunity when the Eastern & Midlands Railway, serving King's Lynn, Fakenham, Norwich, Cromer and Yarmouth and a railway works at Melton Constable, fell on hard times in 1889.

Together with two other constituent companies, the Bourne & Lynn Railway and the Peterborough, Lynn & Sutton Bridge Railway the newly-formed M&GNJR had a route mileage (mainly single track) of 183 miles making it the largest joint railway operation in Britain. The company owned an assortment of locomotives but the stars of the show were certainly the fifteen handsome 4-4-0s built by Beyer-Peacock between 1881 and 1888 for the former Lynn & Fakenham Railway and the later Eastern & Midlands Railway. The

> **DID YOU KNOW?**
>
> The only part of the M&GNJR to escape was the 11½-mile Sheringham to Melton Constable section, but even this succumbed to the 'Beeching Axe' in 1964.

M&GN's locomotive livery was an attractive yellow ochre until 1922 when a new dark brown livery was introduced; passenger carriages were finished in a teak colour. In 1936 the LNER took over the running of the railway and introduced Class 'K2' 2-6-0s and ex-GER 'Claud Hamilton' 4-4-0s to replace the ageing Beyer-Peacocks. Under British Railways the fairly new Ivatt 4MT 2-6-0s became the mainstay of motive power on the system until closure in 1959.

Too slow

As a cross-country railway the M&GNJR provided a vital connection between the Midlands and the North and East Anglia. Goods traffic in both directions was heavy, so was holiday traffic from the Midlands and the North to the seaside resorts of Norfolk during Summer Saturdays. With its long single track sections speed was never one of the railway's main attributes and, following World War II, competition from road transport and the changing habits of holidaymakers led to a dramatic drop in traffic. In 1958, years before Dr Beeching arrived on the scene, the British Railways Committee, looking to reduce its mounting losses, recommended complete closure of the system. Despite an outcry from local supporters the 'Muddle & Get Nowhere Railway' closed on February 28, 1959 and its loss has been mourned ever since.

I'm All Right Jack!

Railway unions – the story of ASLEF and the NUR (**N**o **U**se **R**ushing)

Associated Society of Locomotive Engineers and Firemen (ASLEF)

Although comparatively small in numbers, the members of ASLEF have always been among the elite of railway employees. Comprising engine drivers and firemen, the union was born out of a dispute in October 1879 when the GWR cut the wages and extended the working hours of their longest serving engine drivers and firemen. Receiving no support from the then recently-formed Amalgamated Society of Railway Servants (ASRS) a total of 56 drivers and firemen got together and formed the Associated Society of Locomotive Engineers and Firemen (ASLEF) in February 1880. By 1884 membership had reached 1,000; 20 years later it had grown to 12,000 members and the union had achieved a cut in working hours for these elite men. Although often expressing solidarity with other unions ASLEF has always remained proudly independent and self-sufficient and today has a membership of over 18,500.

The National Union of Railwaymen (NUR)

Before the formation of unions in the 1870s, life for a railway worker in Britain was very dangerous – hundreds were killed in accidents every year, many of these deaths caused by the long hours that they were asked to work. The modern idea of 'Health & Safety' did not exist and passengers' lives were also being put at risk. Although railway employees had at times tried to form workers' associations these were always suppressed in their infancy by the all-powerful railway companies. The first railway union to be recognised was the Amalgamated Society of Railway Servants of England, Ireland, Scotland and Wales which came into being in 1871. Initially membership was small and did not include drivers and firemen who later formed their own union, the Associated Society of Locomotive Engineers and Firemen (ASLEF). By the turn of the century the ASRS was powerful enough to help found the fledgling Labour Party but got into trouble when using union funds to support parliamentary representation.

In 1913 the ASRS merged with two other railway unions – the General Railway Workers' Union and the Pointsmen and Signalmen's Society – to form the National Union of Railwaymen. Then with a total membership of 267,000 it certainly became a force to be reckoned with especially during the strike-torn years in the 1920s. Just prior to nationalisation of the railways in 1948 membership had risen to a peak of 462,000 - from then on the numbers declined due to railway closures which peaked in the 1960s. The NUR's last General Secretary, Jimmy Knapp, was a gruff ex-railway signalman from Ayrshire who played a central role in the merger of his union with the National Union of Seamen in 1990 – this new union is the National Union of Rail, Maritime and Transport Workers (RMT for short) which currently has a membership of 80,000 from almost every sector of the transport industry.

BRITISH RAILWAYS

RULES IS RULES

SOME JOLLY RULES FOR OBSERVANCE BY BRITISH RAILWAYS' EMPLOYEES, 1950

Rule 16, Note (i) – Where women or juniors are employed the Rules and Regulations apply to them as men.

Rule 17 (vi) – station Masters are responsible for a daily inspection of the station, also the cleanliness and neatness of all premises (including closets and urinals), signboards, &c.

Rule 30 – When a horse is used on the railway a man must, on approach and during the passing of any train, hold its head, whether the horse be drawing vehicles or not.

Rule 33 (a) – Clocks at stations and signal boxes must be corrected as may be necessary on receipt of the daily time signal. Which is sent in accordance with the special instructions on the subject. Any defects must at once be reported.

Rule 87 (a) – When a fog or snowstorm occurs during the normal working hours of the men appointed to act as Fogsignalmen they must at once report to the Signalman and take his instructions. The Signalman must advise the Station Master if any Fogsignalman fails to report for duty.

Rule 103 – Where hand or wicket gates are controlled from a signal box, the Signalman must operate the controlling arrangement when necessary to prevent persons crossing the line.

Rule 127 (xvi) – The driver of an engine must have his Fireman disengaged, as far as practicable, when approaching or passing a signal box, so that he also may keep a good look-out for signals.

Rule 127 (xviii) – The driver of an engine must start his train carefully and proceed along the proper line.

Rule 166 – Prisoners and insane persons, with their escorts, must not be placed with other passengers, but in a separate compartment.

Rule 167 – In the event of any passenger being drunk or disorderly, to the annoyance of others, the Guard must use all reasonable means to stop the nuisance; failing which, he must have the offender and any luggage he may have with him removed from the train at the next station. The Guard must obtain the name and address of the offender, and also of one, at least, of the passengers present at the time.

Rule 191 – [Working single line traffic during track repairs or obstruction] A competent person must be appointed as Pilotman, who must wear round his left arm above the elbow, a red armlet with the word "Pilotman" shown thereon in white letter, thus: If this armlet is not immediately available the Pilotman must wear a red flag in the position indicated until the proper armlet is obtained.

STOP PRESS

Railway news, February 1930

* A new electric railway line, 5¼ miles in length, which has been built by the Southern Railway to link up the two residential towns of Wimbledon and Sutton was opened on 5th January. There are six stations on the new line and no fewer than 24 over and under bridges have had to be built.

* The Southern Railway has added greatly to the interest of its locomotives in the Isle of Wight by giving names of island towns and villages to them all. No. W4 'Bembridge' is the most recent addition and was formerly LB&SCR No. 678. She was built at Brighton Works in June, 1880, and when new was No. 78 named 'Knowle'.

* The LNER now have 76 steam rail coaches in regular service on branch lines in England and Scotland. These are very useful for light work.

* The LMS have introduced an entirely new type of luxury coach, on their 'Royal Scot' express, which has been specially fitted with extra large windows giving an uninterrupted view of the countryside. The coaches contain four compartments, decorated in mahogany (Chippendale style), Indian greywood, walnut and oak respectively.

* At the beginning of 1929 the LMS announced that the locomotive-building programme for the year included the construction at Crewe Works of 100 0-8-0 freight engines. The programme was carried through with remarkable precision, and several days before the year closed the last of the series, No. 9599, was completed and sent into service. This engine had been erected in nine days, and its completion marked the achievement of a new record.

* The LNER have placed orders for two 200hp patent geared locomotives for service on the Wisbech tramway. They are capable of being driven fro either end and will be fitted with a governor limiting speed to 14mph.

Days Out

Early excursion trains

As early as the 1840s the idea dawned upon a few enterprising men, of whom Thomas Cook and James Allport became the most famous, that there might be a 'business of travel' in addition to the travel required by business – from this idea grew the excursion train. One of the first excursion trains known in railway history was run on the Midland Counties Railway from Nottingham to an Exhibition at Leicester on August 24, 1840. Apparently the enormous train of nearly 70 carriages carrying 2,400 people passed majestically before the astonished spectators.

During the following years, Cook went on to arrange railway outings from Leicester for temperance societies and Sunday schools, and in 1851 arranged excursions to the Great Exhibition at Crystal Palace for over 150,000 people. Taking a percentage of the cost of railway tickets, his success led to his first foreign adventure in 1855 when he arranged a trip from Leicester to the Paris Exhibition. By the 1860s he was arranging tours further afield to Italy, Egypt and the USA – and he never looked back. Railway excursions and day trips, especially to the seaside, became a popular part of British social life.

Monster railway excursions, especially corporate ones, were run in the late 19th and early 20th century. The GWR annual trip consisted of a succession of trains run to different destinations departing at 10-minute intervals from Swindon.

Drinking & Driving

The story of railway water troughs

By the late 1850s the running of long-distance passenger trains was hampered by the need for regular stops to replenish locomotives with water. To remedy this situation John Ramsbottom, an inventor and then locomotive superintendent of the Northern Division of the London & North Western Railway, designed the water trough in 1860. First fitted on a stretch of the L&NWR North Wales main line at Mochdre to the west of Colwyn Bay, the device consisted of a length of water-filled metal trough, fed from a trackside tank, located in the middle of the track. Water was then collected by a scoop, fitted underneath the locomotive's tender, which could be lowered at speed, thus replenishing supplies without the need for stopping.

Soon water troughs were being fitted at strategic locations on main lines throughout Britain, usually at distances of between 30 and 60 miles apart. The London & South Western

DID YOU KNOW?

The over-filling of water tanks was a great spectacle for observers, as a fountain of water would spurt out of the top of the locomotive. Trainspotters who were standing nearby were often given a good soaking!

Railway was the only major company not to use them, instead choosing to fit their express locomotives with larger capacity eight-wheeled tenders.

By the 20th century their was an extensive network of water troughs on main lines around Britain – by 1930 the GWR had 14 fitted, the majority with a length of 560yds.

Only three water troughs were fitted in Scotland: at Floriston to the south of Gretna Junction and at Strawfrank south of Carstairs, both on the WCML and south of New Cumnock on the ex-G&SWR main line. Early BR diesels such as the Class 40 and 55 were initially fitted with steam-heated boilers, and these continued to replenish supplies from water troughs until the introduction of electrically-heated carriages. Now that water troughs are a dim and distant memory the newly-built Pepperorn Class 'A1' Pacific No. 60163 'Tornado' has been fitted with a larger capacity tender

– an extra 1,000 gallons taking up the space previously used for a scoop mechanism – thus enabling it to complete longer distances while on main line operations.

GWR WATER TROUGHS

Paddington to Plymouth
Between Aldermaston and Midgham
Between Frome and Westbury
Between Durston and Creech St Michael
Between Exminster and Starcross

Paddington to Bristol and S Wales
Between Pangbourne and Goring & Streatley
Between Keynsham and St Anne's Park
Between Badminton and Chipping Sodbury
Between Severn Tunnel Junction and Magor
Between Ferryside and Carmarthen Junction

Oxford to Worcester
Between Charlbury and Ascott under Wychwood

Paddington to Birmingham Snow Hill
Between Ruislip & Ickenham and Denham
Between Aynho and King's Sutton
Between Hatton and Lapworth

Shrewsbury to Newport
Between Bromfield and Ludlow

Victorian Blood, Sweat and Tears

The building of the Settle & Carlisle Railway

One of the major feats of Victorian engineering, the Settle & Carlisle route, beloved by steam enthusiasts across the world, was the last major mainline to be built in this country without the help of mechanical diggers. This heavily engineered route through wild terrain was born out of the Midland Railway's desire to reach Scotland by its own tracks. Receiving Parliamentary approval in 1866 the scheme nearly foundered before construction work had begun due to a financial crisis and a run on UK banks – apparently there's nothing new about this!

Engineered by John Sydney Crossley, work finally commenced on building the 72-mile line in 1870 – the statistics are staggering.

* Both the schedule for completion and final costs over-ran by at least 50%.
* An enormous workforce of around 6,000 navvies, housed in remote and rudimentary camps, caused mayhem with their drunken violence. Hundreds died through accidents and smallpox.

* From the south the first 15 miles of line to Blea Moor were built at a ruling gradient of 1 in 100.
* The summit of the line, at Ais Gill, is 1,169ft above sea level.
* 13 tunnels were built, of which the longest is Blea Moor with a length of around 1½ miles.
* 23 viaducts were built, of which the longest is at Ribblehead with 24 arches and a length of 440yds and the highest, at Smardale, is 131ft high.

The line was opened fully in 1876 and remained a vital Anglo-Scottish rail link until the 1960s when it was listed for closure in the 'Beeching Report'. Despite the ending of through trains and a rundown of services the S&C clung on to life until 1984 when it was announced that the line was to be finally closed. Following public outcry and a well-orchestrated national campaign the Government refused closure in 1989 – the rest is well known with much-needed repairs of the bridges and tunnels and an upsurge in traffic along with regular steam-hauled specials the Settle & Carlisle must rate as one of the most exciting railway journeys in Britain.

All Amenities

Britain's railway hotels

The provision of hotels by railway companies in the UK dates back to the very early days of rail travel. During the 19th century over 100

had been built, many actually adjoining the station they served, such as the famous Royal Station Hotel in Hull, the Caledonian Hotel at Princes Street station in Edinburgh and the largest, the Great Western Royal Hotel at Paddington. Hotels were also opened at railway-connected ports such as Dover, Newhaven, Fishguard and Holyhead, at seaside resorts such as St Ives, Morecambe, Hunstanton and Ayr and at golfing centres such as Gleneagles, Dornoch and Turnberry. The GWR's Manor House Hotel at Moretonhampstead, Devon, and the LMS's Welcombe Hotel at Stratford-upon-Avon were the height of luxury when opened in 1929 and 1931 respectively, while the rebuilt art-deco Midland Hotel at Morecambe, designed by Oliver Hill with sculpture by Eric Gill, became

AMERICAN BAR, MIDLAND HOTEL, MANCHESTER.

an architectural icon after it was reopened in 1930.

Perhaps one of the most famous railway hotels was the Midland Hotel in Manchester, which was regularly used by American cotton traders. It was built next to MR's Central station and opened in 1903.

By 1948 the number of railway-owned hotels had shrunk to around 35 and many of these were in a run-down state after the privations of World War II. Following Nationalisation of the railways the hotels were run at various times by the British Transport Commission, British Transport Hotels and the British Railways Board until they were individually sold in the early 1980s. Albeit with different names, for example the Caledonian Hilton in Edinburgh, the Hilton London Paddington and the Landmark London in Marylebone, many have since been refurbished and restored to their old glory. One of the most famous, the art-deco Midland Hotel at Morecambe has recently reopened its doors following years of neglect and a subsequent major refurbishment.

Railway Walks

A selection of Britain's best closed railways

Thousands of miles of railway lines were closed down following the implementation of the Beeching Report in the 1960s. Since then many have been converted to footpaths and cycleways, the latter mainly by the charity Sustrans. Here are some favourites.

The West Country

The Camel Trail – Wadebridge to Padstow

The Tarka Trail – Barnstaple to Torrington

Yelverton to Princetown

The Somerset & Dorset – Glastonbury to Edington and Bridgwater

The Isle of Portland

Southern England

Camber Tramway – Rye to Camber

Cole Green to Hertford

North London – Ally Pally branch

Three Bridges to East Grinstead

The Cuckoo Line

Wales

Caernarfon to Afonwen

North Wales branches – Bethesda, Dyserth and Holywell

Upper Wye Valley through Rhayader

Barmouth Junction to Penmaenpool

Central England

Wye Valley – Tintern to Monmouth

Horncastle branch

Manifold Valley

Monsal Trail – Buxton to Rowsley

North Staffs – Leek to Rushton Spencer

Wirral Way

Kidsgrove to Etruria

Ironbridge to Coalport

Cromford & High Peak trail

Tissington Trail

East Anglia

Southwold Railway

The Spa Trail – around Woodhall Spa

Lincoln to High Marmam

Sutton-on-Sea branch

Northern England

Border Country – around Kielder

Across the Fells – Cockermouth to Penrith

Yorkshire Coast – Staithes to Whitby

Over the Pennines 1 – Stainmore and Barnard Castle

Over the Pennines 2 – The Woodhead Route

Morecambe Promenade to Lancaster

The Mining Line – the Rosedale branch

Scotland

Glen Ogle – Callander to Killin Junction

The Great Glen to Fort Augustus

The Waverley Route – Hawick to Riccarton Junction

The Paddy – New Galloway to Gatehouse of Fleet

Morayshire Coast – Elgin to Banff

The Fish Route – Fraserburgh and Peterhead

Spey Valley – Dufftown to Craigellachie

Bog Off!

The Irish turf-burner experiment

Following his eleven-year term as Chief Mechanical Engineer for the Southern Railway the innovative locomotive designer Oliver Bulleid moved to Ireland where he became the CME for the newly-formed Córas Iompair Éireann (CIE/Irish Railways) in 1949. Faced with an acute shortage of coal – the Republic had virtually no coal reserves and imports during and immediately after World War II had slowed to a trickle – Bulleid's first task was to solve the vexed shortage of motive power on CIE. Early dieselisation became a priority and by the early 1950s imported diesels were soon replacing the clapped-out vintage steam locomotives.

Bulleid was not only a radical innovator but also possessed what one can only describe as extremely imaginative lateral thought! He had already experimented with the unique 'Leader' Class of steam locomotive

during his latter years as CME of the SR but Nationalisation had killed any further development of this futuristic locomotive. Once in Ireland (a country with virtually no coal reserves) Bulleid came up with a brilliant idea of using the country's seemingly unlimited supply of indigenous peat reserves to fuel a steam locomotive. He first experimented by converting K3 Class 2-6-0 No. 356 to a turf-burning loco – modifications were extensive and included a screw-feed mechanical stoker, twin Crosti pre-heaters and a Franco-Crosti boiler. The pre-heaters on each side of the boiler looking very much like torpedo tubes coupled with the

absence of a chimney made this a very strange looking machine indeed. Steaming qualities were initially appalling but in true Irish style a forced-draught fan was later added and powered by an old Leyland bus engine mounted on a wagon behind the tender!

Spurred on by this experiment Bulleid went ahead with the design for a modern turf/oil-burning locomotive. Numbered CC1 it was built at Inchicore Works in Dublin and externally looked similar to his double-ended box-shaped 'Leader' Class of the SR. With a length of 60ft and a driving cab at each end the loco had an 0-6-6-0 wheel arrangement similar to the 19th century double Fairlies of the Festiniog Railway in North Wales. The firebox and boiler were mounted centrally between the cabs and the fuel bunker and water capacity were located at each end. Trials started in the Dublin area in 1957 but with the retirement of its inventor a year later and the mass-dieselisation of CIE already underway the locomotive was shunted into a siding at Inchicore never to steam again. Sadly this unique piece of Irish railway history was scrapped in 1965.

We've Run Out of Coal

The story of British oil-fired steam locomotives

Until the mass introduction of diesel locomotives in the 1950s Britain's railways depended on a regular supply of good quality steam coal to keep the trains running. Fortunately Britain has always been well endowed with such fuel and it was only during periods of industrial unrest or Arctic weather conditions that railway companies temporarily converted some of their steam locomotives to oil-burning.

The first oil-fired steam locomotive in Britain, appropriately named 'Petrolea', was built by James Holden for the Great Eastern Railway in 1893. Its success led to 100 suburban and express locomotives being built for the railway until the cost of waste oil rose to a prohibitive level and the experiment was ended.

During the prolonged coal miners strikes of 1912, 1921 and 1926 coal was in very short supply and many locomotives were temporarily

converted to oil-burning. Apart from the obvious increase in costs when importing fuel from abroad, oil-burning locomotives were generally cleaner to operate and were more efficient. The largest number of British steam locomotives converted to oil-burning occurred early in 1947 when the country was hit by one of the coldest winters on record. Heavy snowfalls and freezing weather caused roads and railways to be blocked. Coal supplies, already low following the privations of World War II, couldn't reach power stations which were then forced to shut down. The UK not only suffered mass power blackouts but also severe food shortages. Faced with this crisis and to keep the railways running the Labour Government drew up emergency plans to fund the conversion of 1,200 steam locomotives to oil-burning. Faced with the looming coal shortage the GWR, under its CME F W Hawksworth (see page 79) had already begun experimenting with converting examples of 2-8-0 freight locos, 'Halls' and 'Castles'. In typical British fashion the oil conversion scheme soon collapsed as the country did not have enough foreign exchange to purchase the oil!

In more recent times both the Festiniog Railway with their double-Fairlies and the newly-opened Welsh Highland Railway with their Beyer-Garratts have converted coal-burning locomotives to oil-burning – this time as an economy measure when the cost of coal far outstripped the cost of imported oil.

The Railway Navvy

The hard life of a Victorian railway builder

Before the introduction of mechanical steam shovels (known as 'steam navvies') and other heavy excavating equipment in the late 19th century, Britain's railways were carved out of the landscape by men using picks and shovels. The men at the 'coal face' were called navvies, an abbreviation of 'navigator' which was first applied to describe men engaged in the construction of works for inland navigation, or canals. When canals gave way to railways the name was used to describe the same class of men, whose employment was but little different under the new conditions. A 'nipper' was the generic term given to any boy employed in the construction of a railway. Often housed in remote temporary camps, life for the navvy was very hard and many died from accidents and disease.

The navvy was roughly classified under two headings – the navvy proper and the tramp navvy. The former was a respectable member of the community who enjoyed good health and was a good companion. In connection with his work he travelled all over the country and if he was industrious and reliable was usually promoted to a ganger.

The tramp navvy was very different. He was considered to be a less desirable person, a poor unscrupulous specimen who was addicted to drink and was more often than not in need of a thoroughly good bath and disinfecting. Some of these individuals tramped the country, working in a gang for a day or so then living riotously for as many days as their wages would last – during the building of the Settle & Carlisle line in the 1870s (see page 68) the Midland Railway even brought in bible readers to try and curb drunken violence among these men. Finding themselves 'stoney-broke' they would move on to the nearest job and repeat the same tactics. So often were these men without money that there was an unwritten law amongst them that if any out-of-work tramp finds a former mate working in a gang, he was certain of receiving a shilling to help him on his way.

Swindon's Last Great Man

F W Hawksworth – the last Chief Mechanical Engineer of the GWR

Frederick W Hawksworth was born in Swindon in 1884 and joined the GWR in 1898. After working his way up the corporate ladder to the company's drawing office he was appointed Chief Locomotive Draughtsman at the time of the introduction of the 'King' Class locos in 1927. When his famous boss, Charles Collett, retired in 1941 Hawksworth was appointed as Chief Mechanical Engineer. This was a difficult time for the GWR with World War II in full swing and shortages of good quality coal adding to their problems.

Hawksworth assembled a team of 100% GWR men and by 1944 had introduced the 'Modified Hall' Class 4-6-0s which were a notable development of Collett's 'Hall' Class and considered a resounding success. Although plans for a powerful Pacific type loco never got beyond the drawing board the period 1945-47 was busy with the introduction of new powerful 'County' Class and improved 'Castles' with four-row superheaters. Despite being two-cylinder engines the 'County' Cass was certainly a break away from GWR tradition with their high-pressure Stanier '8F' boiler and 6ft 3in driving wheels.

Other loco types introduced under Hawksworth were the '1600' Class and '9400' Class 0-6-0 pannier tanks (the latter with taper boiler) and the '1500' Class 0-6-0 pannier tank, the latter the only locos designed by the GWR with Walschaerts valve gear.

Following Nationalisation in 1948 Hawksworth remained in control at Swindon but was now responsible to the new Railway Executive. He retired at the end of 1949 and died at the age of 92 in 1976.

Just the Ticket

The life and times of a humble railway ticket

Nearly one hundred years before the advent of computerisation and buying tickets online the supply and collection of the humble railway ticket presented massive logistical problems for Britain's railway companies.

Some British railway companies printed their own tickets, for instance the Great Northern Railway had its own stationery stores in Holloway, while others contracted printing firms

> **DID YOU KNOW?**
>
> By the early 20th century around 1,200,000,000 passenger journeys were made every year over the railways of the UK.

such as Waterlow & Sons. Printed tickets then cost railway companies between 1s 3d and 1s 6d (6.5p-7.5p) per thousand, and a million of them weighed a ton. The successive numbering of the tickets from 0001-9999 and their subsequent dating in the press before being passed through the booking office window by a clerk also offered protection against fraud. In those days tickets were usually handed in at the ticket barrier of the arrival station but the story didn't end there!

Collected tickets were carefully packed up and sent off without delay to the audit office at the company's headquarters where was a large room totally devoted to ticket-sorting. In this office a team of young men and women (the latter were favoured as they were defter and more

methodical) sorted every collected ticket into its proper series. In this way the mistakes made by booking office clerks and collectors were brought home to them by means of a report periodically made by the audit accountant to the superintendent of the line as to numbers missing or irregularly issued. Fraud on the part of travellers was often detected by vigilant ticket-sorters – a favourite trick was to buy a ticket to the next station down the line but travel much further and hope for a lax ticket collector at the end of the journey!

After the tickets were sorted they were destroyed by a cutting machine and their remains sent for recycling – nothing was wasted and many thousands of ticket-sorters were kept manfully employed around Britain.

What a Boer!

How the London & South Western Railway saved the British Empire

Until the London & South Western Railway came to the rescue in 1892 Southampton Docks was in deep trouble. Within a few years the railway company had modernised the moribund concern including the installation of 25-miles of railway, new hydraulic cranes, new warehouses, new graving docks (amongst the largest in the world), thousands of feet of sheltered deep water quayage and the finest cold storage installations in Europe. By the early 20th century goods traffic was up by 90%, coal traffic over 100% and passenger traffic by 70%. However its proximity to the great military centres of Southern England also gave it supreme importance for the embarkation and disembarkation of troops and their supplies during the Second Boer War. It is no exaggeration to say that during this period the L&SWR materially helped to save the British Empire from the terrible calamity of the over-running of Natal by the Boers between 1899 and 1902

THE EMPRESS DOCK, SOUTHAMPTON, L. AND S. W. R.
This photograph was taken at the time of the Joint Naval and Military Expedition, September, 1904, and shows some of the transports berthed.

– an opinion voiced by Lord Kitchener on his return from South Africa.

Joint naval and military manoeuvres were also mounted by the government in 1904 to test the capabilities of Southampton Docks in an even more striking way. On September 5, in connection with this expedition, no less than ten transports totalling 90,000 tons gross were simultaneously berthed in Empress Docks and along the ocean quays. Transported to the docks by the L&SWR the force consisted of 12,000 officers and men, 2,900 horses, 61 guns, 315 transport, engineer and ambulance wagons and 55 landing boats. The work commenced at 7am and by 3pm nine out the ten transports had finished loading and got away – the 10th transport was delayed for two hours by a steering fault.

The disembarkation test on September 16 was even more successful. All ten transports returned simultaneously, commencing at 9am, and in an hour they had all been berthed, 9,000 of the troops and many of their horses were entrained at the docks immediately on disembarkation and the remainder marched away with the cavalry, guns and wagons. The whole expedition was clear of the docks by 3pm – only six hours after the arrival of the first ship. The Duke of Connaught, who was present with this expedition, personally expressed thanks to Mr Williams, the L&SWR's superintendent at the docks, his appreciation of the arrangements and facilities by which the remarkable feat had been achieved. During later conflicts, in particular the two World Wars, Southampton Docks once again showed its vital military importance – thanks to the far-sighted planning of the L&SWR during the late 19th century.

No Win, No Fee

Early 20th century bogus injury claims against railway companies

During the early 20th century Britain's railway companies were some of the biggest joint-stock corporations in the country. In view of their size they were also fair game to smart people who could circumvent the railway authorities and turn the weaknesses of the latter to financial advantage for themselves. Born by an Act of Parliament each railway company stood above the ordinary law but required the services of legal advisers from day one. Most of the principal companies set up their own legal departments using salaried staff to deal with the numerous legal questions that arose in connection with railway management. Within these departments were sub-departments dealing with Parliamentary work, conveyancing and Common Law – the latter dealing with claims made upon railway companies for personal injuries to passengers, or damage or loss of freight.

There were many faked-up claims for injury against railway companies – some were successful but many others were not. One of the most extraordinary was of a coloured man who somehow managed to assume a ghastly livid green hue, claiming that it was caused by an injury he sustained while travelling on a train. In court medical men and lawyers were all deceived and a lump sum compensation was awarded to him for his 'incurable' injuries – he was never seen again!

Not all claims were successful – one bogus fraud upon a railway company in 1904 resulted in the claimant being prosecuted for perjury and sentenced to a term of hard labour. He was the only passenger out of several hundreds who were travelling on a train from Euston who complained of a physical injury sustained during a slight bump during a shunting operation. Apparently his injury stopped him from running several 'lucrative businesses' that he owned and made a claim for damages of £5,000 (an enormous amount for the time). However, enquiries by the L&NWR's solicitor's department discovered that he had a history of bankruptcy and fraud and he was arrested just before he was to flee the country to North America. He was tried at the Old Bailey and sentenced to nine months hard labour.

All large railway companies employed detectives to shadow individuals who were suspected of making bogus claims. One such claimant who was shadowed was supposed to have become an invalid during an 'accident' but was found to have assisted a lady friend to move from one set of lodgings to another on the same night of the claimed incident, had spent that night at her new rooms, had amused the baby and had apparently taken part in the mysterious disappearance of the contents of a bottle of whisky! His claim was dismissed in court.

A RAILWAY SOLICITOR AT WORK.

The late Mr. C. H. Mason was appointed Chief Solicitor of the London and North-Western Railway Company in 1883, at the early age of thirty-two, and held that important office with distinction until his sudden death at the close of 1902. He was distinguished as an athlete as well as learned in the law.

The most notorious case of fraud against a railway company was by Leopold Redpath, head of the registration department of the Great Northern Railway in the 1850s. While earning a salary of £250 a year he pocketed more than £200,000 by creating fictitious stock in the company's registers and selling it through brokers on the Stock Exchange. Found guilty at the Old Bailey in January 1857 he was sentenced to transportation to Australia for life – one of the last criminals to undergo this punishment.

From Cradle to Grave

Victorian railway towns

One of the most striking features of railway development in Britain was the way in which large numbers of men, employed by a single company, were grouped together to form the majority of the male population of the towns in which they lived. Formerly small villages before the advent of the railway, towns such as Swindon, Crewe, Wolverton, Horwich and Eastleigh owed their existence to the fact they were great railway centres.

By the end of the 19th century Horwich, in Lancashire, and Eastleigh, in Hampshire, were two of the youngest railway towns to come into existence. When the Lancashire & Yorkshire Railway's mechanical engineering works were established at Horwich in 1887 the population of the small town was under 4,000; by 1904 it was 16,000 of which around 10,500 were dependent on the employment provided by the railway company. As in Eastleigh, housing was provided for this influx by private enterprise but the railway companies invested in well-equipped technical and leisure institutes for their employees.

The Horwich Institute was built with a grant of £5,000 from the L&YR with a gift from a director's widow paying for additional mechanical and engineering laboratories and a gymnasium. A cottage hospital was also paid for by another director. In 1890 about 11 acres of land were given by the railway company for use as a recreation ground for associated cricket, football, bowling and tennis clubs.

The London & South Western Railway had opened a carriage and wagon works at Eastleigh in 1891 and in the space of 15 years the small village had grown into a railway town of 9,000 inhabitants. At the same time the L&SWR had purchased 200 acres of land adjoining the existing works where they opened a new locomotive works in 1910, transferring about 2,000 more men and their families from the old works at Nine Elms in London.

Normally, houses in railway towns were not owned by railway companies but built by private enterprise and rented to the employees. One exception was the Glasgow & South Western Railway which built a model village in 1896 for its locomotive staff and families at Corkerhill, near Glasgow. The population of 800 people was lodged in 120 houses, and allotments and a Railway Institute were later added. Religion was also important and Sunday services were conducted in the large hall of the Institute by members of the Railway Mission. There was also a Sunday School at Corkerhill, with an average attendance of 110 children, and a Bible Class for young men and women, with an average attendance of 70.

MECHANICS' INSTITUTE AND TECHNICAL SCHOOLS, HORWICH, L. AND Y. R.

Southern Railway Famous Trains

The two crack trains of the SR

The Golden Arrow

During the late 19th century, years before the advent of air travel, the only way to travel between London and Paris was by boat train. Compared to the current Eurostar service through the Channel Tunnel, the journey was leisurely and involved a ferry journey between Dover or Folkestone and Calais. In 1906 the London Brighton & South Coast Railway (LB&SCR) introduced luxury Pullman cars and within a few years these were included in their boat trains from Victoria station. Soon after the formation of the Southern Railway in the 1923 Grouping an all-Pullman boat train was introduced and in 1929 it was officially named the 'Golden Arrow' – on the French side of the Channel the corresponding train between Calais and Paris was called 'Flêche d'Or'. In 1936 the SR built a luxury ferry, the 'Canterbury', for the sole use of its first class passengers on the London to Paris route. The ship was also fitted with rails on the cargo deck which carried through coaches of the luxury 'Night Ferry' sleeper train between the two capitals.

The outbreak of World War II brought an end to the service, only returning again in April 1946. Bulleid's new air-smoothed 'Merchant Navy' and light Pacific locomotives based at Stewart's Lane shed were now in charge of the train which, by 1951, had been augmented by the introduction of new Pullman cars and was temporarily renamed the 'Festival of Britain Golden Arrow'. Locomotives hauling the train were grandly adorned with a long golden arrow on each side and on the smokebox door. Two of the first batch of brand new BR Standard 'Britannia' Class locos, No. 70004 'William Shakespeare' and No. 70014 'Iron Duke' were specifically allocated to Stewarts Lane in 1951 to haul the upgraded 'Golden Arrow', a job they continued to do until they were transferred to Longsight, Manchester, in 1958.

During the 1950s the popularity and speed of air travel between London and Paris spelt the end for this luxury train which was now made up of 1st Class Pullman cars and standard 2nd Class stock. Electric haulage by BR-built (Class 71) Bo-Bo locos (E5000-E5023) was introduced in June 1961 and continued until September 1972 when this famous train ceased to run.

The Atlantic Coast Express

Until the GWR opened its shorter route from Paddington to Plymouth (via Westbury and Castle Cary) in 1904 there was immense competition between that company and the rival London & South Western Railway to provide the fastest service between the two cities. The latter's 11am departure from Waterloo to Plymouth was the forerunner of what became known as the 'Atlantic Coast Express', which by 1927 under Southern Railway management contained through carriages to many destinations in Devon and North Cornwall – the name was selected in a competition of SR employees, the winner being a guard from Woking.

Trains between Waterloo and Exeter had always been forced to stop at Salisbury following a serious derailment at the station in 1906. It was here that locos were usually changed but with the introduction of the 'Lord Nelson' 4-6-0s in 1927 through running became the order of the day. However, due to the lack of water troughs on the SR, the Salisbury stop continued to be included until the end of steam to take on water and a crew change. By the outbreak of World War II the down 'ACE' consisted of through coaches to Sidmouth, Exmouth, Ilfracombe, Torrington, Bude, Padstow and Plymouth.

Halted by World War II the 'ACE' resumed service soon after the end of the war with Bulleid's new 'Merchant Navy' Pacifics in charge of the heavily loaded train as far as Exeter. Beyond this the various portions were taken on to their destinations behind his new 'Battle of Britain/West

Country' Class light Pacifics. By 1952 the train had become so popular with holidaymakers that it departed from Waterloo in two separate portions. During its peak in the late 1950s extra relief trains, headed by the rebuilt 'Merchant Navy' locos, were also added to cope with the amount of traffic. Timings were continually improved until 1961 when the 171¾-mile journey from Waterloo to Exeter Central was scheduled to take only 2hr 56min – this included stops at Salisbury and Sidmouth Junction.

Although increased car ownership in the early 1960s can partly be blamed on the downfall of the 'ACE' the other contributing factor came in 1963 when all lines west of Salisbury came under Western Region control. Anxious to stamp their authority on their erstwhile competitors, the end was swift and painful. The last 'ACE' ran on 5 September 1964 and soon downgraded 'Warship' diesel hydraulics took over services on what was to become a secondary route – much of the line west of Salisbury was singled and branch lines in Devon and North Cornwall, much loved by the poet John Betjeman, were closed.

'ACE' 1963

SUMMER SATURDAY TIMINGS FROM WATERLOO:

10.15 with through coaches to Ilfracombe and Torrington

10.35 with through coaches to to Padstow and Bude

10.45 to Seaton with through coaches to Lyme Regis

11.00 with through coaches to Torrington and Ilfracombe

11.15 with through coaches to Plymouth, Padstow and Bude

Foreign Travels

Flying the flag for Britain

GWR 4-6-0 No. 6000 'King George V'

Built at Swindon in 1927, the 'King' Class locos were the GWR's response to the Southern Railway's powerful 'Lord Nelson Class 4-6-0s which had been introduced a year earlier. With a tractive effort of 40,300lb/f the 'Kings' became the most powerful 4-6-0s in Britain. The first of the Class, 'King George V', entered service at the end of June, 1927 and was allocated to Old Oak Common shed and was soon at work on the GWR's premier train, the 'Cornish Rivera Express'. At the beginning of August the loco, along with broad gauge 2-2-2 'North Star', was shipped from Cardiff to Baltimore, USA, to represent the GWR at the Baltimore & Ohio Railway's Centenary Exhibition which took place between 24 September and 15 October. After appearing at the Exhibition, where the 'King' was

fitted with a commemorative brass bell and cabside plaque, the loco and her GWR crew, Driver Young and Fireman Pearce, made runs between Baltimore, Washington and Philadelphia. Returning to the UK in November 1927 the 'King' went on to haul the principal expresses out of Paddington until withdrawal from service at the end of 1962. Fortunately this historic loco was saved for preservation and, in 1971, became the first preserved steam locomotive to be approved for mainline running since the end of steam on BR. It is now a static exhibit at the York Railway Museum.

LMS 4-6-0 No. 6100 'Royal Scot'

Built as No. 6152 'The Royal Dragoon Guardsman' at Derby in 1930 this loco permanently swapped identities with the first engine of this class in 1933 when it was sent with a train of carriages to the Century of Progress Exposition in Chicago. Fitted with a large headlamp the engine and train then covered over 11,000 miles over the railroads of Canada and USA and was visited by over 3 million people. On return to the UK the loco remained on mainline duties on the West Coast Main Line between Euston and Glasgow until being withdrawn by BR as No. 46100 in October 1962. Fortunately the loco was saved for preservation, firstly by Billy Butlin and then by the Bressingham Steam Museum in Norfolk, and has recently returned to steam on preserved railways and main lines around the UK.

LMS 4-6-2 No. 6220 'Coronation'

The loco that was sent to represent Britain at the 1939-40 New York World Fair was actually built as No. 6229 'Duchess of Hamilton' at Crewe in 1938. Her number and nameplate was swapped with the first engine of the class for the duration of what turned out to be a much longer than planned visit. Fitted with a streamlined casing and accompanied by eight matching crimson-lake and gold striped carriages, the

loco was also fitted with a headlight, brass bell and special couplings for the duration of her stay in North America. After completing a tour of over 3,000 miles around the continent, the loco and her train was exhibited at the World Fair but became stranded in the US following the outbreak of World War II. The loco was finally shipped back to the UK in 1942 where she reverted back to No. 6229 'Duchess of Hamilton'. Used as an officer's mess, the carriages only returned back to the UK in 1946. The loco was de-streamlined in 1947 and withdrawn in 1964. Since then she has been preserved and was returned to mainline working order. Currently the loco is being fitted with her original streamlined casing and will be exhibited alongside ex-LNER . No. 4498 'Mallard' at York Railway Museum.

LNER 4-6-2 No. 4472 'Flying Scotsman'

Although this famous LNER 'A3' Class 4-6-2 did not travel abroad until after preservation, 'Flying Scotsman' has certainly attracted much public and media attention in more recent years. Following withdrawal by BR as No. 60103 in 1963 the loco was purchased for £3,000 by Alan Pegler who restored her back to her original condition. With the addition of a second tender the loco worked rail tours around Britain in 1968 including a non-stop run between London and Edinburgh. In 1969 the loco embarked on a promotional tour of the USA for which it was fitted with a headlamp, bell and cowcatcher. Initially a success, the visit came to grief in 1972 when Pegler became bankrupt and the loco was only returned to the UK in 1973 when Sir William McAlpine stepped in to save it.

In 1988 the 'Flying Scotsman' travelled to Australia to take part in bi-centenary celebrations and while there covered more than 28,000 miles, including a run across the Nullarbor Desert from Sydney to Perth. On return to the UK the loco faced an uncertain future when mounting restoration costs led to its sale to Dr Tony Marchington in 1996. By now there was much public outcry about this famous locomotive's future and it was finally bought by the National Collection in 2004 where it is now undergoing a complete rebuild in the NRM workshop at York.

Return to Riccarton Junction

Britain's most remote railway community

The Border Union Railway (later known as the Waverley Route) between Edinburgh and Carlisle and the Border Counties Railway between Riccarton and Hexham both opened throughout on 1 July 1862. As part of the North British Railway's empire the lines served a sparsely-populated hill-farming region on both sides of the Anglo-Scottish border. The junction between the two lines was at Riccarton, renamed Riccarton Junction in 1905, a remote and windswept spot in the Cheviot Hills that grew into Britain's most remote railway community.

As an important railway junction and interchange station the facilities at Riccarton included a two-road engine shed, turntable, coaling facilities, gas plant, smithy, two signal boxes, a carriage shed and extensive siding for goods trains. With no road links to the junction the NBR built a railway village for its employees – drivers, firemen, shunters, cleaners, gangers, booking clerks and porters - and their families.

The railway village included the station master's house, 30 terraced houses for the workers and their families, a school and schoolmaster's house, a post office and grocery shop and a public house. At its height the population of Riccarton reached 120 people, all of whom were cut off from the outside world apart from their occasional forays by train to Hawick or Carlisle. The grocery shop, a branch of the Hawick Co-operative Society, was located on the island platform where a red telephone box was also later installed.

Doctors had to travel to Riccarton by train from Hawick or Newcastleton and if hospital treatment was required the patient was sent by train to Carlisle.

Riccarton ceased to be a junction in October 1956 when the branch line to Hexham was closed and by 1963, when a forestry track was opened up to the village, the writing was on the wall for the 'Waverley Route'. In that year closure of the line was recommended in the 'Beeching Report' and with closure of the school the remaining children had to travel by train to schools in Newcastleton or Hawick. The end finally came on 6 January 1969 when trains ceased to run over the line and Riccarton Junction closed for good.

Since then the large site at Riccarton Junction has been overtaken by Nature and most of the buildings have long since gone. To the north is Whitrope, now the headquarters of the Waverley Route Heritage Association. From the car park here it is possible to walk south along the trackbed for two miles through forestry plantations to the eerily silent Riccarton Junction. Still inaccessible by road, Riccarton Junction is one railway pilgrimage worth making. Here the island platform has been partially restored with station nameboard and (disconnected) red telephone box. A few ruined railway buildings, included the former NBR schoolhouse, still remain while a short length of recently relaid track and an old goods guards van complete the picture. To the south the trackbed leads through more forestry plantations to Steele Road where the former station building is now a private residence.

Trains Don't Run Here Anymore

Lost train journeys on the London Midland and Eastern Regions of BR

A trip along the last main line to be built in Britain - the Great Central Railway – by now with seriously depleted services and a misleading timetable. The GCR was the only route in the UK to be built with a Continental loading gauge and no level crossings – its closure in 1966,

MIDLAND AND EASTERN REGIONS

WEEKDAYS, SUMMER 1962

LONDON MARYLEBONE TO BACUP

Itinerary

London (Marylebone)	dep. 8.38am
Nottingham (Victoria)	arr. 11.43am
Nottingham (Victoria)	dep. 2.00pm
Chesterfield Central	arr 3.01pm
Sheffield (Victoria)	dep. 5.45pm
Manchester (Piccadilly)	arr. 6.44pm
Manchester (Victoria)	dep. 7.50pm
Bury (Bolton St)	arr. 8.14pm
Bury (Bolton St)	dep. 8.20pm
Bacup	arr 8.54pm

only 68 years after opening, was seriously short-sighted. We continue our journey across the Pennines to Manchester on the Eastern Region's Woodhead route – which was electrified in 1954, closed to passengers in 1970 and completely in 1981. Our journey ends with a trip to Bacup via Bury – part of this route, from Bury to Rawtenstall, is now the East Lancashire Railway. What a jolly day out – 229 miles in all behind steam, electric and dmu - but a trip that is no longer possible.

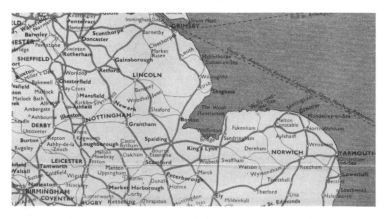

NB: By this date the GCR was being deliberately run down in readiness for closure and the LMR timetable gives the arrival at Sheffield Victoria as 5.11pm – only 16 ¾ miles from Chesterfield Central! Departure time from the latter station was not shown in the timetable.

Our 205¾-mile journey, mostly by diesel multiple unit, takes just under 12 hours to complete. It takes in the delights of soon-to-be-closed rural Norfolk branch lines, the seaside resorts of Wells-Next-The-Sea and Hunstanton, the lengthy East Lincolnshire line through Boston and Louth and a ferry across the River Humber to Hull where we can spend the night before tackling the North Eastern Region. Again, the vast majority of this mainly rural route through Eastern England has long since disappeared.

When Paddington Station Closed

The day that thousands of people tried to escape London

During the Blitz of London by the Lutwaffe in 1940–41 the capital's inhabitants at least had some advance warning of attacks by the use of air raid sirens enabling them to shelter in bunkers. However, in 1944, the latter stages of the war brought an even more terrifying experience when Hitler's V1 and V2 rockets started falling without warning on the capital. Driven by fear and the need to escape, thousands of Londoners descended on Paddington station on July 29 hoping to catch a train out of town.

Despite appeals from the GWR's General Manager, Sir James Milne, the Minister of War Transport refused to allow extra coaches to be provided on trains to cater for this influx. Bursting at the seams, Paddington was closed for three hours and enormous queues built up along the length of Eastbourne Terrace. Exits from the Underground were also closed and many people were given first aid by St John's Ambulance and at the GWR's first aid post. Although there was also congestion at Euston and Waterloo the refusal by the Ministry to alleviate the situation at Paddington was a national disgrace and led to questions in Parliament where it was asserted that British citizens were treated like cattle!

While this was all going on the GWR took it upon themselves to assemble 16 relief trains at Old Ok Common – no mean feat in itself. But without Ministerial approval the trains could go nowhere! By now completely at his wits end, Sir James Milne threatened to take the matter to a higher authority (Winston Churchill?) – this threat seemed to work and approval was soon given by the authorities to run the relief trains. With their 16 trains already assembled the GWR soon cleared the vast crowds and took them to safety.

STOP PRESS

Railway news, December 1932

* Feed-water heaters of the A.C.F.I. pattern have been fitted to three standard 0-8-0 mineral engines, Nos. 9672-74, engaged on heavy duties of the L&NWR section of the LMS.

* At Swindon Works steady progress has been made with the order for 20 tank engines of the 2-6-2 '6100' class and it is expected that all will be finished before Christmas. A number of 'Kings' have recently been through the shops for a thorough overhaul after a long and arduous season dealing with heavy holiday traffic. Some speedometers of different types have been tried recently on several of the 'Kings' with interesting results.

* The scrapping of the 4-4-0 'County' class has been proceeded with at Swindon and the class is now almost extinct. Several of the 'County' tanks ('2200' class) have also been cut up during this year.

* Another 'Claughton' class 4-6-0, No. 5966, has recently been reconstructed as a 3-cylinder 'Baby Scot' at Crewe and is now stationed at Camden Shed.

* The steelworks at Crewe Works have been closed down permanently. There is no intention to abandon Crewe as a centre of railway activity and certain subsidiary workshops are to be concentrated there.

* The electric services on the SR main line between London and Three Bridges are operating very satisfactorily. The through electric services to Brighton and Worthing are to come into operation on 1st January. Meanwhile the interposing of the full steam service to Brighton, Worthing, Reigate and other places, with the new electrics is a decided handicap but there will be many regrets at the disappearance of the long-familiar steam locomotive.

The Infernal Combustion Engine

Early experiments with diesel and gas turbine technology

Even before World War II problems with coal supplies caused by industrial unrest had led many American railroads to invest heavily in diesel electric technology as a replacement for steam traction. Apart from a few faltering steps in the 1930s Britain lagged behind until after World War II when two of the 'Big Four' railway companies built experimental diesel electric main line locomotives and the GWR dabbled with gas turbine technology. Although the gas turbines led up a cul-de-sac, the diesel electric prototypes paved the way for the introduction of British Railways first generation of main line diesels in the late 1950s.

The GWR's experiment with gas-turbines

Seeking an alternative source for main line motive power in the 1940s the GWR decided to investigate gas-turbine technology. Their reasoning for this decision was that a gas-turbine locomotive could produce enough power to equal their 'King' Class 4-6-0 whereas they would need two diesel-electric locomotives to do the same job. Delayed by World War II the GWR finally ordered the prototype gas-turbine locomotive No. 18000 in 1946. The A1A-A1A loco was built in Switzerland by the Swiss Locomotive Works and Brown, Boveri and was delivered to British Railways in 1950. A slightly more powerful Co-Co loco, No. 18100, was built by Metropolitan-Vickers of Manchester and delivered a year later. Operating main line services out of Paddington both locos proved to be unreliable and heavy on fuel – No. 18100 was withdrawn in 1958 and later converted to run as a test bed 25kv AC electric loco. In this new guise it ran as E1000 (later E2001) until it was withdrawn from service in

1968. No. 18000 was withdrawn in 1960 and returned to Europe where it was used, firstly as a test bed (minus its gas-turbine equipment) by the International Union of Railways and, secondly, as a static exhibit in Vienna. It was later returned to the UK for preservation and is currently on display at Barrow Hill roundhouse.

The London Midland & Scottish Railway's prototype diesel-electric locomotives

First off the mark after World War II, the LMS were the first to introduce main line diesel electric locos. Designed by H G Ivatt, CME of the LMS, two Co-Co locos, Nos 10000 and 10001 were built at Derby Works with the first one being delivered towards the

end of 1947, only two months before Nationalisation. No 10001 followed later in 1948. Powered by English Electric units both locos had a power output of 1,600hp and, because of their low power output compared to the 'Coronation' Pacifics, had to work in multiple when hauling heavy passenger trains. To enable this a connecting corridor was fitted in the front nose of each loco. After operating on the Midland and West Cast Main Lines the pair were transferred to the Southern Region in 1953 where their performance was able to be compared with the more powerful Bulleid diesel-electric locos Nos. 10201-10203. The five locos were permanently transferred to the LMR in 1955 where they were allocated to Willesden depot. For some years they made regular appearances working in multiple on the WCML hauling expresses such as the 'Royal Scot.'

No. 10001 was withdrawn in 1962 and 10000 was withdrawn in 1966. Neither of these ground-breaking machines was preserved despite their considerable contribution to the design of BR's first generation diesel-electric locos.

The Southern Railway's prototype diesel-electric locomotives

Designed by Oliver Bulleid for the Southern Railway these slab-fronted main line diesels were actually built by BR after Nationalisation. With English Electric power units the first two locos (Nos 10201 and 10202), with a power output of 1,750hp, emerged from Ashford Works in 1950 and were soon put to work hauling expresses out of Waterloo. These two locos were joined in 1953 by the two LMS diesels, Nos 10000 and 10001, for joint performance trials. A third Bulleid-designed loco, No, 10203, with a power output of 2,000hp, was built at Brighton in 1954. All five locos were permanently transferred to the LMR in 1955 where they were allocated to Willesden and operated trains on the WCML. All three of the SR locos were withdrawn in 1963. None has been preserved.

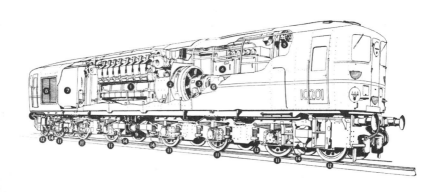

Know your Train

Steam locomotive head codes

Head codes, usually white painted oil lamps denoting the type of train being hauled, were first fitted to the front of locomotives in the mid-19th century. Their purpose was to help signalmen identify the type of trains that were in their section of line. A red oil lamp was also fitted to the brake van or carriage at the rear of the train. The head codes were standardised by the Railway Clearing House (RCH), a body originally set up in 1842 to manage and allocate revenues collected by the hundreds of pre-grouping railway companies.

Revised head codes were introduced by the RCH in 1923 but there were still some variations for daylight hours – both the SR and LNER used plain white discs.

To further identify the train, both the Southern Railway and GWR fitted train reporting numbers to the smokebox door of their steam locos, a practice which continued under British Railways. These reporting numbers evolved during the 1960s into four-character headcodes which were displayed on roller blinds in indicator boxes at each end of main line diesel and electric locomotives. The practice ended in 1976 following the introduction of centralised control and the removal of most manually-operated signal boxes.

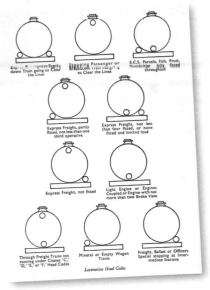

Locomotive Head Codes

Diesel and Gas Turbine Prototypes for BR

1960s private enterprise prototypes

In the race to gain lucrative contracts for building British Railways' new fleet of main line diesels in the 1950s and '60s, several leading locomotive manufacturers produced designs for evaluation by their potential client. Some had a very short life and one disappeared without trace behind the Iron Curtain.

Deltic (DP1)

Forerunner of the Class 55 diesels, the 'Deltic' prototype, was a familiar sight on both the ECML and WCML. Also known as DP1 it was built by English Electric at their Vulcan Foundry in 1955 and was finished in a striking powder-blue

livery with cream side stripes and speed whiskers. The twin-Deltic marine engines had a combined power output of 3,300hp. It was withdrawn in 1961 and has since been preserved as part of the National Collection.

Falcon (D0280)

Built in 1961 by Brush as a second-generation lightweight diesel-electric loco, the one-off experimental D0280 'Falcon' was fitted with twin Maybach diesels, Finished in a striking lime green and brown livery 'Falcon' saw trials on the ER and LMR before being repainted in two-tone green and allocated for a time to Bath Road diesel depot, Bristol and operated main line services to Paddington. It was eventually sold to BR in 1970 for its scrap value and was subsequently rebuilt at Swindon as No. 1200. Due to its non-standard design it was withdrawn in 1975 and subsequently scrapped.

GT3

This strange-looking 4-6-0 gas turbine locomotive was built by English Electric in 1961. Resembling a slab-sided steam locomotive, GT3 also had a tender and required turning at the end of each journey. Finished in red livery the loco was tested on the Great Central Main Line and on the WCML before being returned to its manufacturer the following year. It was finally scrapped in 1966.

Lion (D0260)

Resplendent in gleaming white livery, prototype mainline diesel D0260 'Lion' took part in trials for a new BR Type 4 diesel fleet. Built in 1962 by the Birmingham Railway Carriage & Wagon Company at Smethwick, the loco was withdrawn at the end of 1963 when BR ordered a fleet of Type 4 (Class 47) diesels from Brush Traction.

DP2

Similar in outline to the 'Deltic' Class 55 diesels, English Electric prototype DP2 was the test-bed for the company's Type 4 diesels (later Class 50) introduced in 1967. Built at Vulcan Foundry in 1962 the loco saw service on the ECML and WCML until it was withdrawn following a serious accident at Thirsk in July 1967.

Kestrel (HS4000)

Prototype Co-Co diesel HS4000 'Kestrel' was built by Brush Traction in 1968. It was powered by a 4000hp Sulzer engine and finished in a yellow ochre and dark brown livery. Following trials it was refitted with lighter bogies and went into service on the ECML. The loco was withdrawn in 1971 and sent to Russia as a research vehicle and has not been seen since!

Peacetime Horrors

Britain's worst peacetime rail crashes

Harrow & Wealdstone October 8, 1952

Involving two collisions between three trains, the worst peacetime rail crash in Britain occurred at Harrow & Wealdstone station on the main line out of Euston during the morning of October 8, 1952. At 8.19am a stationary stopping train from Tring to Euston was hit in the rear by 'Coronation' Class 4-6-2 No. 46242 'City of Glasgow' travelling at 50-60mph with the Perth to Euston sleeping car train – the loco was not fitted with an Automatic Warning System and its driver had failed to observe both 'caution' and 'danger' signals to the north of the station. Wreckage was strewn across the down main line and this was hit seconds later by a Euston to Liverpool and Manchester express travelling at 50mph and double-headed by 'Jubilee' Class 4-6-0 No. 45637 'Windward Isles' and 'Princess Royal' Class 4-6-2 No. 46202 'Princess Anne'. The latter engine had only emerged from Crewe two months earlier after being rebuilt as

a conventional locomotive from the steam turbine 'Turbomotive'. The resulting scene of death and destruction was horrific – 112 people lost their lives (including the driver and fireman of the train that caused the accident) and 340 were injured. 'City of Glasgow' was repaired and returned to service but both 'Windward Isles' and 'Princess Anne' were scrapped.

Lewisham December 4, 1957

The second worst peacetime rail crash in Britain occurred near St Johns station in Lewisham. In thick fog, a Charing Cross to Hayes electric train was halted by a red signal shortly after passing St Johns station – its last carriage left standing underneath a railway flyover. In the meantime, on the same line, the much-delayed express from Cannon Street to Ramsgate was powering towards Lewisham behind 'Battle of Britain' 4-6-2 No. 34066 'Spitfire'. The thick fog meant that neither driver nor fireman saw the yellow caution signals, and only when the red danger signal was spotted at the end of St Johns station did the driver attempt an emergency stop – all in vain as the heavy express piled into the rear of the electric train at 35mph. Not only were the rear coaches of the latter train completely demolished, but the lead coach of the express was derailed bringing the railway viaduct crashing down on the next two coaches. To add to this scene of carnage, a train about to cross the viaduct narrowly avoided being brought down into the wreckage. 90 people were killed and 173 injured. As at Harrow & Wealdstone, although driver error was mainly to blame, the lack of an Automatic Warning System on the locomotive was a major contributory factor in the crash.

No. 34066 was repaired and returned to service. It became one of the last unrebuilt Bulleid Pacifics to remain in service until withdrawal in September 1966.

Let the Train Take the Strain
The story of car-carrying trains

Before the age of the car, privately-owned horse-drawn carriages were regularly transported around Britain by train. They were usually conveyed in special carriage trucks attached to scheduled passenger trains. By the beginning of the 20th century early motor cars were also being carried in the same manner, with the Midland Railway being one of the first companies to offer this service. In Scotland, with the opening of the Ballachulish branch in 1903, road vehicles were carried across the Connel Bridge from Connel Ferry station to North Connel on a specially adapted goods wagon until 1914, when the bridge was then resurfaced to accommodate both road and rail traffic.

A scheduled car-carrying service was introduced in 1924 by the GWR between Severn Tunnel Junction and Pilning High Level as an alternative to the erratic Aust Ferry across the River Severn. Passengers were conveyed in separate carriages while the cars travelled on open bogie trucks attached to the rear. Cars were usually filthy at the end of their journey after being carried through the dripping tunnel by a steam engine!

The scheduled service ended in 1966 with the opening of the Severn Bridge.

The Motorail services, as they were known, started in 1955 with the introduction of an overnight London to Perth service by the Eastern Region of BR. A daytime service between London Holloway and Edinburgh was introduced in 1960 and, within a few years, the network had expanded to include destinations from London such as Stirling, Inverness, Fishguard and St Austell. Outside London there were services between Manchester with Dover, Sutton Coldfield and Inverness, Newcastle and Exeter, Newcastle and Dover and York and Inverness. The majority of the trains ran overnight and were made up of sleeping cars attached to either flat car transporter wagons or converted end-loading GUV covered wagons. Cars were loaded on and off the train via an end-loading dock at a station – the one at the west end of Reading station could be seen for many years after falling into disuse. The only purpose-built Motorail terminal opened at Kensington Olympia in London in 1961 – this remained in use until 1981.

Motorail services peaked in the late 1970s with around 30 destinations served but the opening of new motorways and the increasing reliability of cars led to a gradual decline in routes.

British Artics

The Beyer-Garratts of the LMS, LNER and the Welsh Highland Railway

LNER CLASS U1 2-8-0+0-8-2

Articulated Beyer-Garratt steam locomotives had been built for railways of the British Empire by the Manchester company of Beyer-Peacock since 1909 (see page 38). The first to be built for a British railway company was the unique LNER Class U1 2-8-0+0-8-2 No. 2395, which was introduced in 1925. This massive loco was specifically designed to bank heavy coal trains over the ex-GCR Woodhead route in South Yorkshire and spent most of its life allocated to Mexborough shed. With a length of over 87ft and a tractive effort of 73,000lbs the Class U1 was both the longest and most powerful steam locomotive of its time in Britain.

Following a brief sojourn as a banker on the Lickey Incline south of Birmingham in 1949, the loco, now renumbered 69999, returned to the Woodhead route until electrification of that line in the early 1950s made it redundant. Returning to Bromsgrove for the second time, this time fitted with a large electric headlight, the loco spent its last three months as a banker up the Lickey Incline before withdrawal at the end of 1955.

LMS 2-6-0+0-6-2

As successor to the Midland Railway the LMS was faced with continuing the former company's small engine policy. In short this meant double-heading of all heavy trains including coal trains

southwards from the Nottinghamshire coalfields to London. To overcome this expensive operation the LMS took delivery of three 2-6-0+0-6-2 Beyer-Garratt locomotives from Beyer Peacock in 1927. With another 30 locos built in 1930 the LMS had a large fleet of powerful goods locos for the first time – although slightly longer than the LNER U1 they were significantly less powerful with a tractive effort of just over 45,000lb. The majority of the class, most of which were now fitted with revolving coal bunkers, was allocated to Toton shed in Nottinghamshire where they were employed on heavy coal trains down the Midland main line to North London. Renumbered 47967–47999 in 1948 the class was gradually withdrawn between 1955 and 1958.

Welsh Highland Railway

Recently completely rebuilt and reopened from Caernarfon to Porthmadog the 1ft 11½-in gauge Welsh Highland Railway possesses no fewer than five Beyer-Garratt articulated steam locomotives, which are among the most powerful narrow gauge engines in the world. The oldest, the first of its type to be built, is an 0-4-0+0-4-0 that was delivered to the Tasmanian Government Railways in 1909.

Four larger 2-6-2+2-6-2 locomotives, built between 1937 and 1958, were rescued from South Africa where they once operated on the Alfred County Railway. These 62-ton, 48ft-long monsters are capable of hauling a 12-coach train up 1 in 40 gradients at a speed of 25mph.

Trains Don't Run Here Any More

Lost train journeys on the North Eastern and Scottish Regions of BR

North Eastern Region, Weekdays Summer 1961
Hull to Penrith

273 miles of complete contrasts taking in the scenic Yorkshire coast route through Robin Hoods Bay, the North York Moors line, ECML steam haulage, a couple of hours trainspotting at Darlington and the scenic route across the Pennines to Penrith on a DMU. The train left Hull at 6.55am, with changes at York, Scarborough, Whitby, again at York and then Darlington, arriving in Penrith at 6.35pm. Sadly the Hull to York via Market Weighton line, the scenic Yorkshire coast line and the trans-Pennine route to Penrith have all long since disappeared. The one bright spot is the North York Moors Railway from Pickering to Grosmont which is now a steam-hauled heritage line.

Scottish Region, Weekdays Summer 1964
Stranraer to St Combs

This is a lost journey to end all lost journeys. Apart from four short sections (Dumfries–Carlisle, Edinburgh–Thornton, Leuchars Junction–Dundee–Perth and Kinnaber Junction–Aberdeen) this fascinating route has long since disappeared from the timetable. Admittedly one can still travel by

train from Stranraer to Aberdeen but not by this 445-mile long-lost route. Our train from Stranraer over the wild and remote line across Galloway to Dumfries will be steam-hauled; at Dumfries we travel to Carlisle behind a 'Peak' diesel on the up "Thames-Clyde Express; then follows the highlight of the day, the famous 'Waverley Route' via lonely Riccarton Junction to Edinburgh (probably 'Peak'-hauled too); we are in luck at Edinburgh as there is a through DMU service to Dundee via the picturesque Fife Coast line; on to Perth where we have time for some fish and chips and a quick bunk round 63A before catching the early-morning train to Aberdeen, quite likely to be 'A4'-hauled; the final leg is up the 'Fish Line' to Fraserburgh and then on to our destination at tiny St Combs where we can stretch our legs on the beach.

TIMETABLE

Itinerary

Stranraer (Town)	dep. 8.05am
Dumfries	arr. 10.34am
Dumfries	dep. 10.42am
Carlisle	arr. 11.22am
Carlisle	dep. 1.46pm
Edinburgh	arr. 4.34pm
Edinburgh (Waverley)	dep 5.10pm
Dundee (Tay Bridge)	arr 8.04pm
Dundee (Tay Bridge)	dep. 9.04pm
Perth	arr. 9.38pm
Perth	dep. 12.57am (next day)
Aberdeen (via Forfar)	arr. 3.20am
Aberdeen	dep. 6.55am
Fraserburgh	arr. 8.30am
Fraserburgh	dep. 8.50am
St Combs	arr 9.10am (exhausted!)

Let Us Pray

Three famous men of the cloth who loved railways

Bishop Eric Treacy (1907–1978)

Born and educated in London, Eric Treacy became a Deacon in the Church of England in 1932 and was Vicar of Edge Hill, Liverpool from 1936 to 1940. Taking up photography as a hobby in the 1930s he was soon drawn to Lime Street Station and the photogenic qualities of steam railways. His first published photograph was of a 'Royal Scot' leaving Lime Street with an express which appeared in the Liverpool Post. In 1935 he became a member of the Railway Photographic Society and soon gained a reputation for his atmospheric railway shots. By the outbreak of World War II he had become an established railway photographer of the railway scene in north-west England with his photographs taken at Shap are still considered to be some of the finest ever taken.

Following World War II when he was a military Chaplain, Eric Treacy moved on to become Rector of Keighley and soon discovered the photogenic qualities of the Settle & Carlisle line – his photographs taken during this period capture the raw beauty of steam locomotives working hard in a wild and desolate landscape at locations such as the 'Long Drag' up to Blea Moor, Ribblehead Viaduct and Ais Gill Summit. His photographs were soon appearing in a growing number of railway magazines and books – his first major book was *Steam Up*, which was published in 1949.

Throughout his clerical career Eric Treacy not only pursued his love of railway photography but also got an insight into railway life, meeting footplatemen and taking footplate rides. From 1949 to 1961 he was Archdeacon of Halifax and in 1968 was made Bishop of Wakefield. Despite this high office his love of railways never diminished, and with the end of steam in 1968 he turned his attention to the less romantic diesel scene. This passion for railways continued after his retirement in 1976 with his appointment to the Council of the Friends of the National Railway Museum in York. Eric Treacy died suddenly at Appleby station on his beloved Settle & Carlisle line in 1978 while photographing preserved '9F' 2-10-0 No. 92220 'Evening Star'. Fittingly, his collection of 12,000 photographs are now part of the NRM's archive.

Reverend Wilbert V Awdry (1911–1997)

From an early age Wilbert Awdry, son of the Vicar of Ampfield, near Romsey in Hampshire, couldn't fail to have a love of railways. His father, known as 'Railwayman Parson' had been interested in railways all his life and a move to Box in Wiltshire, within sight and sound of the GWR main line, in 1917, firmly cemented young Wilbert's growing passion for them. Educated at Wycliffe Hall, Oxford, Wilbert Awdry was later a teacher in Jerusalem before becoming an Anglican priest in 1936. In 1940 he became a curate in Kings Norton, Birmingham and it was here that his famous 'Railway Series' of children's books was born.

In 1942 his son, Christopher, was suffering from measles and to entertain the poor lad his father made a small, wooden model engine which he later named 'Thomas'. At Christopher's suggestion Wilbert made up stories about an imaginary railway on the Island of Sodor – its star was, of course, 'Thomas the Tank Engine'. His first book, *The Three Railway Engines* was illustrated by Reginald Payne and published in 1945. New titles followed annually until 1972, by which time 26 had been published. The amazing success of these books never dazzled Wilbert and, in retirement, he enjoyed his time with involvement in the railway preservation movement and by creating model railway layouts and showing them at exhibitions up and down the country, often assisted by his friend Rev 'Teddy' Boston – the latter was immortalised as the 'Fat Clergyman' in Awdry's books!

Although Wilbert Awdry died in 1997 his imaginary railway, characters and locomotives live on – an enormous commercial success, 'Thomas the Tank Engine' has spawned a lucrative worldwide business empire in recent years with TV and film spin-offs, merchandising and 'Days out with Thomas' events on heritage railways.

Reverend 'Teddy' Boston (1924–1986)

A close friend of Rev Wilbert Awdry, in 1960 'Teddy' Boston became Rector of Cadeby and Vicar of Sutton Cheney in Leicestershire. Immortalised in the Rev Awdry's Railway Series as the 'Fat Clergyman', 'Teddy' Boston filled his rectory with model

railways, the grounds with a passenger-carrying steam operated 2ft-gauge light railway and founded the annual Market Bosworth Steam Rally. The mainstay of steam motive power on the line was provided by 0-4-0 saddle tank 'Pixie' which Boston bought in 1962 from a local quarry. After his death in 1986 the Cadeby Light Railway was kept open by his widow until 2006 when it finally closed.

One-offs

The story of six unique British steam locomotives

Caledonian Railway 4-2-2 No. 123

Known as the 'Caley Single' this elegant single-wheeler was built for the Caledonian Railway by Neilson & Company in Springburn, Glasgow in 1886. In the same year the loco was exhibited at the Edinburgh International Exhibition where it won a gold medal. In service the loco was employed hauling express trains on the West Coast route to Carlisle before taking on the important task of hauling the Directors' saloon in the 1920s. The loco became LMS No. 14010 in 1923 and was withdrawn for preservation in 1935. Returned to working order in the late 1950s, No. 123 spent a few years hauling enthusiast specials before becoming a static exhibit in the Glasgow Museum of Transport.

GWR 4-6-2 No. 111 'The Great Bear'

Designed by G J Churchward and built at Swindon in 1908 'The Great Bear' became the first Pacific type locomotive in Britain and the only one to be to be built for the GWR. More of a publicity stunt, the locomotive and its eight-wheeled tender was not a great success as the heavy axle loading restricted its operations to the Paddington to Bristol route. Retaining its number of 111 the loco was rebuilt as a 4-6-0 'Castle Class' in 1924 and renamed 'Viscount Churchill'. It remained in service until withdrawal in 1953.

MR 0-10-0 'Big Bertha'

Only two 0-10-0 (known as 'decapod') steam locos were built for service in Britain. One was a tank engine built for the Great Eastern Railway in 1902, the other was a tender locomotive, nicknamed 'Big Bertha', designed for the Midland Railway by James Clayton specifically for use as a banker on the 1 in 37 Lickey Incline south of Birmingham. Built at Derby in 1919 No. 2290 weighed 107 tons and its 10 driving wheels were driven by four cylinders. Complete with electric headlight 'Big Bertha' was renumbered 58100 by British Railways in 1948 and remained in service as a Lickey banker until 1956 when it was replaced by a new BR Standard 9F 2-10-0.

LMS 4-6-0 No. 6399 'Fury'

Based on the frames of Fowler's 'Royal Scot' class 4-6-0, this unique high-pressure locomotive was built in 1929 by the North British Locomotive Company. Despite a fatal accident in 1930 when a high-pressure tube burst, the loco underwent four years of trials but never entered service. It was rebuilt in 1935 with a normal Stanier taper boiler and became No. 6170 'British Legion'. As No. 46170 the loco was withdrawn by British Railways in 1962.

LNER 4-6-4 No 10000 'Hush-Hush'

Designed by Nigel Gresley for the LNER, the Class 'W1' was the only 4-6-4 tender locomotive to operate in Britain. Its unusual features included a high pressure marine type water boiler built by Yarrow & Co. Under a cloak of utmost secrecy No. 10000 was part-assembled at Doncaster before being completed at Darlington at the end of 1929. There then followed six months of tests and modifications before the loco entered service in June 1930 – between that date and August 1935 the loco was in and out of Darlington Works many times for repairs and further modifications, the last visit including the fitting of a Kylchap exhaust in May 1935. No. 10000 finally emerged from Doncaster at the end of 1937 with a conventional boiler and a streamlined casing similar to the 'A4' Class. Entering BR service the loco was re-numbered 60700 in 1948 and withdrawn in June 1959.

LMS 4-6-2 No. 6202 'Turbomotive'

Designed by William Stanier, the 'Turbomotive' was a modified 'Princess Royal' Class 4-6-2 built in 1935. Using turbines instead of cylinders the loco was considered a great success but fell foul of British Railways' management in 1949 when it required a new turbine. As No. 46202 the loco was eventually rebuilt as a conventional loco in 1952 and named 'Princess Anne' after the Queen's daughter who had been born two years earlier. After only two months in service the loco was involved in the Harrow & Wealdstone crash on October 8, 1952 (see page 106) and subsequently scrapped. It was replaced in 1954 by BR Class 8 4-6-2 No. 71000 'Duke of Gloucester'.

BR 4-6-2 No. 71000 'Duke of Gloucester'

Designed by R A Riddles (see page 122) this unique 3-cylinder Standard Class 8 loco was built at Crewe in 1954. With its design based on the 'Britannia' Class 7 Pacifics, No. 71000 differed in having modern Caprotti valve gear but suffered in service due to high fuel consumption and poor steaming resulting from draughting problems. It was withdrawn in 1962 after only eight years of service, and languished at Dai Woodham's scrapyard at Barry until 1975 when it was bought for preservation. Since then it has been completely rebuilt with modifications that have resulted in a highly efficient and powerful steam locomotive.

STOP PRESS - 4

Railway News, December 1930

* The last of the first batch of the SR 'Schools' class, No. 909, 'St Paul's', has been stationed at Nine Elms shed for experimental purposes. It has been fitted with a shelter and the apparatus necessary for taking indicator diagrams and making other tests, and has been tried on a variety of services.

* Work has begun on the extensions of the Piccadilly Tube Railway from Hammersmith to Northfields, and from Finsbury Park to Cockfosters. It is estimated that work will be found for about 20,000 men.

* The building of the new series of engines of the three-cylinder 4-4-0 'Shire' class is being delayed by the LNER owing to the depression in trade, and they will not be completed by the end of the year as was originally intended.

* The LNER reports that the 'Flying Scotsman' expresses ran non-stop between King's Cross and Edinburgh daily during the 1930 Summer Season without a single case of engine failure. The 132 trips, each of 393 miles without a stop – a world record – were performed without even the slightest defect developing in the intricate and powerful mechanism that constitutes a modern 'Pacific' locomotive.

* The 'Southern Railway Magazine' points out that if all the milk churns that were dealt with at Clapham Junction Station during one year were stood side by side, they would stretch from Waterloo to Guildford! For the 12 months ended June, 1930, 1,176,295 churns were dealt with.

* In the course of the present year 176 stations on the four big British railway systems have been closed for passenger traffic. Of these, 88 are on the LNER; 60 on the LMS; 24 on the GWR; and 4 on the Southern Railway. This drastic action has been taken in the interests of economy.

Know your Engine

British steam locomotive wheel arrangements

Devised by an American, Frederick Whyte, the Whyte Notation for classifying steam locomotives first came into use at the beginning of the 20th Century. The system is based on groups of wheels separated by a dash – eg a tender locomotive with a two-wheeled front bogie, six driving wheels and a rear two-wheeled bogie is classified 2-6-2. A tank engine has a T (side tank) suffix following the wheel arrangement – eg 0-6-0T. Variations on the latter are PT pannier tank, ST saddle tank, WT well tank. Articulated Garratt locomotives have a + sign between each wheel arrangement – eg 2-6-2+2-6-2.

Certain popular wheel arrangements were also given names, eg 4-4-2 Atlantic, 2-6-0 Mogul and 4-6-2 Pacific.

Tender Engines		Tank Engines	
oOO	2-4-0	OO	0-4-0 T
ooOO	4-4-0	oOO	2-4-0 T
oooOOo	4-4-2	OOo	0-4-2 T
OOO	0-6-0	OOoo	0-4-4 T
oOOO	2-6-0	oOOo	2-4-2 T
oOOOo	2-6-2	ooOOo	4-4-2 T
ooOOO	4-6-0	OOO	0-6-0 T
oooOOOo	4-6-2	OOOo	0-6-2 T
OOOO	0-8-0	oOOOo	2-6-2 T
oOOOO	2-8-0	OOOoo	0-6-4 T
OOOOO	0-10-0	oOOOoo	2-6-4 T
oOOOOO	2-10-0	ooOOOo	4-6-2 T
		OOOO	0-8-0 T
		oOOOO	2-8-0 T
		oOOOOo	2-8-2 T
		ooOOOO	4-8-0 T
		OOOOoo	0-8-4 T

Setting Standards

R A Riddles – the last great British Chief Mechanical Engineer

Robert Arthur Riddles was born on May 23, 1892 and was a premium apprentice with the London & North Western Railway at Crewe Works between 1909 and 1913. He then became a fitter at the Works before serving with the Royal Engineers during World War I. After the war, during which he was seriously injured, he returned to

DID YOU KNOW?

Riddles drove 'Coronation' on much of its North American tour due to the illness of its regular driver.

Crewe where he became responsible for overseeing engine sheds and other locomotive department buildings and the construction of the new erecting shop at the Works. Following this he was promoted to head the production department and was mainly responsible for the reorganisation of Crewe Works in 1925–1927.

During the 1926 General Strike Riddles became a volunteer driver – a task which included a run from Crewe to Carlisle with a Scotch express. This practical experience was certainly put to good use when he was appointed as CME of the embryo British Railways in 1947.

On completion of his task at Crewe, Riddles was then moved to Derby to head a similar reorganisation of the former Midland Railway Works. In 1933 he became Locomotive Assistant to William Stanier and two years later was promoted to Principal Assistant during which period he was closely involved in the design and construction of the 'Coronation' Class Pacifics until being transferred to Glasgow as Mechanical & Electrical Engineer in 1937. In the same year he was closely involved with the record-breaking test run of No. 6220 'Coronation' when the loco achieved 114mph south of Crewe before accompanying this famous streamlined locomotive on its tour of North America in 1939.

World War II was Riddles' great break – first becoming Director of Transportation Equipment for the Ministry of Supply and then, in 1941, as Deputy Director General, Royal Engineer Equipment. In this role he was not only involved in the design and production of Bailey bridges and the D-Day Mulberry Harbours, but also the design and construction of hundreds of the WD 2-8-0 and 2-10-0 locomotives. In 1943 he returned to the LMS as Chief Stores Superintendent and expected to be promoted to CME on the sudden death of Charles Fairburn in 1945. Instead George Ivatt received that appointment and Riddles got second-best as Vice-President.

With Nationalisation of the railways looming, Riddles was appointed as Chief Mechanical & Electrical Engineer of the newly-formed Railway Executive in 1947. In this role he was responsible for the design and construction of 999 steam locomotives for British Railways – three classes of 4-6-2, two classes of 4-6-0, three classes of 2-6-0, two classes of 2-6-2T, one class of 2-6-4T and one class of 2-10-0. Probably the most successful of his designs, 251 of the latter type were built – in 1960 No. 92220 'Evening Star' became the last steam locomotive to be built for British Railways.

Robert Riddles retired in 1953 and died on June 18, 1983.

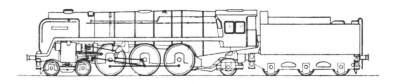

Know your Engine

Main line diesel and electric locomotive wheel arrangements

Unlike steam locomotives, which are classified under the Whyte notation of wheel arrangement, main line diesel and electric locomotives are classified under a variation of the UIC (International Union of Railways) axle arrangement.

Unlike the Whyte notation which counts wheels, the UIC notation counts each pair of wheels, or axles, in the following way:

Capital letters – these signify the number of consecutive driving axles, e.g.
A = single axle, B = double axle, C = triple axle
'o' – this signifies axles that are driven by electric traction motors
Numbers – these signify consecutive non-driving axles

BRITISH DIESEL MAIN LINE LOCOMOTIVES AND THEIR WHEEL ARRANGEMENTS

1Co-Co-1: BR Type 4 'Peak' (Class 44-46), English Electric Type 4 (Class 40).

A1A-A1A: North British Type 4 'Warship' (Class ??), Brush Type 2/3 (Class 31).

B-B: BR/NBR Type 4 'Warship' (Classes 42/43), Beyer Peacock Type 3 ('Hymek'Class 35).

C-C: BR Type 4 'Western' (Class 52).

Co-Co
Brush Type 4 (Class 47), English Electric Type 4 (Class 50), English Electric Type 3 (Class 37), English Electric Type 5 ('Deltic' Class 55), BR Class 56/57/58/59/60/66

Bo-Bo
BR Type 2 (Classes 24/25), Birmingham R. C. & W.Type 2 (Class 26), English Electric Type 2 ('Baby Deltic' Class 23), NBR Type 2 (Classes 21/22/29), English Electric Type 1 (Class 20), Birmingham R. C. & W. Co. Type 3 (Classes 27/33), BTH Type 1 (Class 15), NBR Type 1 (Class 16), Clayton Type 1 (Class 17), Class 67.

Co-Bo: Metrovick Type 2 (Class 28)

A Kind of Hush

LMS experiments with the Michelin Train

Prior to his death in 1931 Andre Michelin, the French industrialist and manufacturer of pneumatic rubber tyres, spent a sleepless night on board a sleeper train – the noise of the steel wheels on the track kept him awake and inspired him to come up with a quieter solution.

The "MICHELINE"—The first Train on Pneumatic Tyres. In commercial use since 1931 : Born of the Michelin Tyre.

As run on L.M.S. Line (Bletchley-Oxford) 1932

Thus was the rubber-tyred train born – not only was it quieter but it was also more comfortable. Early in 1932, following successful tests made with pneumatic-tyred petrol-engined railcars in France, a single railcar was tested by the LMS on the Bletchley to Oxford line. This strange looking vehicle seated 24 passengers, had ten pneumatic-tyred wheels, three pairs in front and two at the back, and was driven by a 27hp Panhard et Levassor sleeve valve petrol engine. The pneumatic tyres, fitted with a metal flange to keep the wheels on the rail, were inflated to $85lb/in^2$ and contained a wooden hoop which kept the wheels on the track if the tyre deflated.

Following their trials on the Bletchley to Oxford line and in the Midlands the LMS then investigated a much larger vehicle. Known as the Coventry Pneumatic Rail-Car it was powered by a 240hp 12-cylinder engine and seated 56 passengers. The driver sat in a raised turret at one end allowing him unobstructed views for running in either direction. Weighing 6.5 tons the 54ft-long railcar also had rapid acceleration with a top speed in excess of 60mph. Trials were carried out in 1935 on the main line between Euston and Leighton Buzzard – following a stop at Watford the next 22¾ miles were covered in 25 minutes with a top speed of 67mph. The non-stop return journey of 40 ¼ miles was covered in 42 ½ minutes.

Index

Acknowledgments

Photographs used in this book have come from many sources. Some have been supplied by the photographers and picture libraries below. Others have been bought on the open market, sometimes with no information about the original photographer. Wherever possible, photographers or collections have been acknowledged, but some images inevitably remain anonymous, despite attempts at tracing or identifying them. If photographs have been used without due credit or acknowledgement where credit is due, through no fault of our own, apologies are offered.

All photographs and illustrations are from the author's collection apart from the following:

J F Aylard: 104
I S Carr: 56
H C Casserley: 49b, 59b, 74, 75, 76, 77, 107
C R L Coles: 101
T G Flinders: 23
Tony Harden: 6
Locomotive & General Photography: 55, 110

Milepost 92½: 7, 43, 46, 47, 48, 69, 116
Ivo Peters Collection: 44, 68
G A Richardson: 53
Getty Images: 51